ALSO BY JANE BRYANT QUINN

Making the Most of Your Money

Everyone's Money Book

JANE BRYANT QUINN

SMART
and
SIMPLE
FINANCIAL
STRATEGIES
for
BUSY PEOPLE

SIMON & SCHUSTER
New York   London   Toronto   Sydney

SIMON & SCHUSTER
Rockefeller Center
1230 Avenue of the Americas
New York, NY 10020

Copyright © 2006 by Berrybrook Publishing, Inc.

SIMON & SCHUSTER and colophon are registered trademarks
of Simon & Schuster, Inc.

For information regarding special discounts for bulk purchases,
please contact Simon & Schuster Special Sales at 1-800-456-6798
or business@simonandschuster.com

Designed by Dana Sloan

Manufactured in the United States of America

10 9 8 7 6 5 4 3 2 1

Library of Congress Cataloging-in-Publication Data

ISBN-13: 978-0-7432-6995-7
ISBN-10:   0-7432-6994-2

For my mother
And in my father's memory

Contents

INTRODUCTION

I've had this book in my dreams for many years. It's the heart and soul of everything I've learned about handling personal money well.

The big thing I've learned is that managing money ought to be simple—and can be, as long as you get the principles right. In the money world, "simple" turns out to be sophisticated. You're skipping the bells and whistles that are a waste of time. If a salesperson shows you a gee-whiz but complicated financial product, you can be sure of two things: You don't need it and it's overpriced. You can get the same result with something easier, wiser, and lower-cost.

I didn't realize this when I started reporting on finance and investments. I dug into details, tried new things, tested every approach. I put my own money (meager savings, back then) into some of the bright ideas and products that the "experts" praised.

Big mistake! As time passed and I tracked results, I saw that those products were mostly guff. On the surface, they looked convincing, exciting, and even no-lose. Underneath, they were just a way of making banks, brokers, and insurance companies rich at my expense.

I learned something else as I went along. A few brilliant people (and companies) were creating—and are still creating—a handful of financial products and strategies that really work. Even better, they're honest, straightforward, and fairly priced. You can put them into effect yourself, certain that they'll serve you well. You don't even have to mind them every minute because they mind themselves.

This short book explains them all. I've chosen the best savings and retirement plans, the best mutual funds, the best mortgages, the best college savings plans, the best life insurance, and the best ways of making them all work. I know their worth because I use them, too. They're combined with a strategy for automatic investing and saving so that you can manage your money in your sleep.

You have other financial options, of course. I've left them out deliberately, to make your planning easier. None are any better than the ones you'll find in the following pages. They're just different and may suit certain special circumstances. They also require more time, effort, and study to produce the results you want. For all the details, see my best-selling personal-finance guide, *Making the Most of Your Money*. (My thanks to Consumers Union, which rated it the best one on the market.)

This particular book is designed for people who don't want a lot of details, just great ideas and reliable results. You're busy, with your job, family, pastimes, friends. You want to do right by your money without having to think about it much. Happily you can. The strategies here are based on sound principles and common sense. Above all, they set you free so that you can get on with all the things that matter more. That's my real dream. A world where you can trust your financial plan enough to forget about it, and give your mind and heart to the joys of life.

Jane Bryant Quinn
New York

SMART AND SIMPLE

FINANCIAL STRATEGIES

FOR BUSY PEOPLE

1. GETTING STARTED

Why Am I Even Reading This,
I Don't Have Time!

I think I can change your financial life, from muddle-along to easy, permanent success. That's why I wrote this book.

"Easy" sounds phony but trust me, it's not. Of all the ways of managing money, nothing beats the simple ways. I'll go even further—the simple ways are not only smart, they're also the most sophisticated. It takes a clear head and a wise eye to distinguish the good from the bad in the confusing world of personal finance. Only the good can make you financially secure.

From experience, I know how much time it takes to find the financial products that work the best, and time is what nobody has today. The path of least resistance carries you toward the usual stuff that the money industry sells—investment, insurance, and banking products with high (and often hidden) fees. They're what most people buy, so you figure they must be okay.

I wish that were so. When you really study this subject, as I have, you learn that what's on offer is mostly mediocre and sometimes downright bad. The products are expensive, which wastes your money. They're often complicated, with risky angles that you didn't know about. If you pick your own investments, you may choose things that don't go together well, leaving big gaps in your security fence. If you buy from brokers and planners who earn commissions, you may find yourself trapped in a poorly performing product that you don't understand. Even your company's 401(k) may be stuffed with losers. Maybe everything will still work out, but maybe not. No wonder so many people feel a little bit anxious about their money, and out of control.

It doesn't have to be this way! Managing money isn't hard as long as you keep it simple. Not only are simple products, er, *simple* to understand, they cost less, gain more in value, and leave you more secure. In this book, you'll find the most straightforward, sensible products and strategies I know—and in case you're wondering, I use them all. In fact, they're all I use.

Why am I so sure they'll lead you to success? Because simple systems fit into our busy daily lives. That's where lots of personal-finance advice falls short. You're expected to morph into some kind of expert—a lover of picture-perfect budgets, a student of stock price/earnings ratios, a sponge for new financial terms. If you could do that—or wanted to—you'd have done it already. Maybe you've even tried, by reading other money-management books. If so, I know what happened. You underlined sentences, made some notes to yourself, and then went to the movies. Maybe you tracked your spending for a couple of weeks before giving up. You thought about fixing your 401(k) but your mind (or gut) still clenched. Given this history, you assume you're a failure—a klutz who'll never be any good at personal finance.

Not true. To start with, you're smart (this isn't a "dummies" book). You're good at your job, wise about your children and friends, and know about stuff that mystifies me—airplanes, synthesized music, quarks, patent law, ultimate Frisbee, cooking (yes, cooking). You're perfectly capable of managing money, if only it interested you. But it doesn't, so you defer, denounce, deny (and worry in the night).

This book understands that. Good financial planning builds from your personality up. To gain control of your money, your strategies have to fit you like a glove, so you know—without fretting—that you're doing the right thing. You need a program you can practically write on the palm of your hand. One that takes into account the distractions and inertia that embody normal life.

Including my normal life. Money is my business but it's not my hobby. I think, talk, and write about personal finance all day. After hours, I want family and friends. I'd rather read a John Grisham thriller than settle in with Sidney Homer's *History of Interest Rates*. All my bills get paid on time and I glance at the monthly totals on my investment statements. I may make a change in my mutual funds (usually later than I should have). Generally, however, money management lies near the bottom of my list. I don't have the time to spend. Well, maybe I have potential time, but I'd rather spend it on things I find more fun. And the same with you.

Happily, you can get away with it. You can give just a nod to your finances and still do better than your friends who play with their money all the time. Playing around leads to mistakes. "Hands off" is one of the easy-money rules that works. The key is to start off right: Buy good insurance and set up an automatic system for saving, investing, and clearing your debts. After that, your finances can run themselves while you get on with the rest of your life.

A HYMN TO THE SIMPLE FINANCIAL LIFE

Most of us can manage wonderfully, using just a few strategies and tools. That sounds crazy at first. All financial advertising tells us we're incredibly special, needing products that have to be tailored to us personally. A smiling "financial adviser"—a wizard, by implication—stands ready to steer you through the mysteries for a fat, though often hidden, fee.

Pooh. The only wizard that Wall Street resembles is the Wizard of Oz. Out front, a mighty voice and megaphone; behind the screen, an ordinary person trying to impress. Financial firms love to make investing look complicated, so you'll need their help. But all good financial advice springs from the same short list of principles that you already know: Save more, borrow less, pay attention to taxes, invest regularly, diversify, limit risk, and hold down fees. You can do that yourself, without a wizard in sight.

Once you start looking into easy ways of managing money, you'll get two big surprises.

First, you don't need discipline. Save your discipline for your diet, where you'll need it more. You can set up your finances so you'll get rich (or at least rich enough) without thinking about it. You can reach this comfortable goal on an ordinary salary, without hitting the jackpot in business or investing in a lucky stock. You don't even need a financial adviser to help. All the tools exist to do the job properly, while you sleep. You just have to trigger them and then yawn off.

The second surprise is how few things you really need. Sure, there are thousands of financial choices out there in Money World, but when you look at them closely you find that they're mostly fluff. It's a world of copycat mutual funds, funds whose high fees will demolish your returns, seemingly safe (but actually risky) investment annuities, costly insurance policies, mortgages that never end—all salable products, but often stupid and sometimes even deceptive. You even have to be careful with useful investments, such as low-fee mutual funds. There are too many to choose from, especially in your 401(k) or Individual Retirement Account, and it's easy to make mistakes. When you can't investigate every investment, or don't have a basis for choosing, you often put off making any choice at all. Or you don't revisit choices you made ten years ago because—as usual—you have no time.

To cut through the clutter and help you make good, new decisions fast, I've made a short list of things that work. They're not money "basics"—this isn't a kindergarten class. Just because something is simple doesn't make it naïve. In fact, this book's investment strategy is pursued by hundreds of major institutions that invest billions of dollars of workers' pension money and college endowment funds. The strategies for insurance and savings are endorsed by top academics and financial planners.

I'm not proposing a cookie-cutter system, with just one plan for everyone. Life is personal. We all make choices with our money. What I'm saying is that the list to choose from—the good list—is surprisingly small.

There are just two little secrets to personal finance. First, *managing money isn't hard.* Sure, you can complicate it, but why would you want to? Lots of evidence proves that the simpler things work better than the alternatives touted by the Great American Financial Sales Machine. Once you've cleared your mind of what Wall Street says, you'll hit on the other little secret: *You don't need what they're selling!* Difficult to believe, I know, but true. You can ignore almost every financial ad you see and everything your friends boast about when they talk money (remember, some of them lie!). This program works better, and with less risk.

YOUR NEW LIFE: GETTING STARTED

You don't have to start by getting organized. If you ever catch me in organization mode (filing bills, cleaning closets, sorting the piles of paper on my office floor), you'll know I have something hard to do that I'm putting off. You'll eventually want to track your net worth and create good financial files, but that can come later. It's best to begin with something that moves the ball down the field right away.

So surprise yourself by discovering what financial products you already have. This might require some excavating. You've probably forgotten some of the choices you made in earlier years. Many spouses and partners don't know what decisions the other has made—not because anything's hidden but because you haven't thought about it much. On the retirement front, you might be ignoring your 401(k) or other investments, crossing your fingers and hoping for the best. But by letting things ride, you give up on the chance of making them better. You might even find that your situation isn't as wiggy as you feared, just not well enough on track. If you truly haven't been doing enough, it's never too late. Or almost never. All you have to do is start.

So . . . make a pile of your latest financial statements—bank accounts (checking and savings), debts (mortgage, home equity line, credit cards, and any other), insurance (life, homeowner's, auto, disability, umbrella—the amount and type), retirement accounts (what the plans are worth and how much you're contributing), any college savings, brokerage house and mutual-fund statements, real estate holdings, and other investments.

List all your debts—the balance, the interest rate, and how much you're paying every month—then set that part of the pile aside (don't even add it up, if that will scare you off).

Now for the interesting part. List all your investments and insurance policies, along with their current value. If you don't know their value, an approximation will do. Next to each item, write down why you own it. Something simple is enough. "I own life insurance to protect my family if I die." Or, "I chose this mutual fund because it's a growth fund and I want my money to grow." Or (be honest, here), "I bought 5,000 shares of Weirdo General because a guy told me it would triple." If you know more, put that down, too. For example, "I chose this mutual fund because I looked it up and it did well over the past five years." If you have no particular reason for owning something on your list, that's fine, too. Just leave it blank.

Or rather, leave it blank for now. This is your starting place. The idea is to fill in the blanks as you proceed, chapter by chapter, through this book. You'll be amazed at how helpful the "why do I own it" question is going to be. Asking it (and working out better answers than you had before) will do three wonderful things. (1) You'll reflect on whether you need that particular item at all (maybe Weirdo General ought to be dumped). (2) You'll nail down, in your mind, what that product is supposed to contribute to your life. (3) You'll start thinking about whether it really meets your goals and, if not, what to substitute. Some of the financial products or services on your current list you'll find you definitely want to keep because they exactly fit your needs. Other things you will probably change because you've found something better.

As you make your decisions, you should record more detailed answers to the question "Why?" For example, instead of saying you own life insurance "to protect my family," you'll write something like the following:

I bought $900,000 worth of term insurance from Neverfail Life Insurance Co. to support my family if I die. I figured that my spouse will need $35,000 per year for 20 years, to supplement his/her salary, plus $100,000 for each child's higher education. At age 55, I'll check to see if I still need coverage and, if so, how much.

Does that sound too complicated? Don't worry, you'll easily figure it out when you read Chapter 4. By recording these details, you'll have more than a mere life insurance policy—you have an insurance *plan*. Here's another example: Next to "401(k)," you might write:

I'm contributing 7 percent of salary. When I get my raise next March, I'll go up to 10 percent.

Bingo, that's another plan. You can tell your computer's calendar to remind you about your decision next March, or write it on the wall or desk calendar you use.

These notes have a very practical purpose. They help you keep track of your thinking process, which will be important when you forget (again!) why you made a particular choice. And don't worry, everyone forgets, me included. That's what happens when you have a busy life. At some point in the future, you'll have a new question about your personal finances. When you check back, this list will put you into the picture right away. It keeps you in control of your money and your plan. If something needs changing, you can pick up from where you left off without starting the "why" process all over again, from scratch. These notes can also be terrifically reassuring if—in the dark of night—you start wondering whether you've done the right thing. Let me say right here, that answer is going to be *yes*. When you've thought about why, you'll almost certainly be on track.

On which track? Toward your goals, of course—so after you've finished this list, start another one headed "Goals." We all have goals, but they generally live only in the backs of our minds. That makes it all too easy to get sidetracked into stuff we hadn't intended. To make things happen, you need to put your goals front and center. Frame the question this way: What are you working *for*? If all your money goes out the door for groceries, credit cards, entertainment, and the electric bill, you're always working for someone else. To work for yourself as well, you should deliberately set some of your income aside for the specific things you want.

So list your personal goals, along with a time frame for achieving each one (don't break your head on the time frames; terms like "soon," "in a few years," and "way out there" will do). The goals labeled "soon" might include a new car, a vacation, a first house, clean credit cards (no consumer debt—what a concept!). "In a few years" might be college tuition or starting your own business. Retirement might be "way out there." It depends on your age and life events.

You're going to find this list a huge help when you reach Chapter 7 and think about how to arrange your savings and investments. For each time frame, there's a perfect place for your money to be.

Pulling together your key financial records and making these two lists shouldn't take more than three or four hours (two, when you know where your records are). *Then* you can go to the movies. If you already have a good filing system, add a file labeled "Goals and Decisions" or some such thing, where you'll put your notes, or keep them in your computer (with a good backup!). If your records are in a jumble, keep the pile you made today in a single place. You can work on your filing system later, as you start to consider what to do.

To make the smart changes you're looking for, you first need to learn the rules of the financial road. It won't take long. The rules are the same for men and women, singles and marrieds, the young and the old. Simple solutions work especially well for spouses and permanent partners who haven't thought about coordinating their finances (or haven't been able to agree). Clarity helps create trust, in yourself and each other. That leads you to a better place.

I'm not promising that you'll end your working life as a millionaire (although that could easily happen, with steady savings and smart investing). I'm not promising that you'll be able to retire at 55 (also possible, but do you really want to?). What I *can* promise is an end to that nagging worry that you've overlooked something, chosen badly, or made a big mistake. You won't be investing blind or overpaying for bad advice. There are plenty of "wrongs" in personal finance, but not on this short list. Using it, you'll be okay—in fact, better than okay. You'll retire with good money and, in the meantime, feel secure with the choices you've made.

Temptation always rears its head. We can't help but dream that, somehow, some financial pied piper can pipe $100 bills into our bank accounts. Somewhere, we think, there exists a genius who'll whisper the secret of tripling our investments in a year. This broker, that newsletter or message board, a "miracle money manager" who supposedly made your cousin a fortune—one of these gurus (you imagine) will put you on easy street. Don't believe it. That's Wall Street legend, urban myth. A few people win the financial lottery, but that's usually luck, not foresight or skill. You can't predict that any particular mutual fund or investment adviser will make it happen. In real life, no one but you can buy your ticket to success.

So it's time to act. Every chapter in this book gives you things to do and ways to do them, to build your financial security. You'll also free yourself from the common fears that come with money decisions. Will you make a big mistake? *No.* Will you understand what I'm talking about? *Yes.* Will you lose your money? *No.* Will you come to see that you're a fabulous manager? Maybe not, but it doesn't matter. This plan manages itself. To beat your normal, human inertia—the urge to leave everything as it is—leave this book on your desk or hall table, so it will give you a kick.

Maybe you won't make these changes because you think I'm nuts. I am, in a way, in my drive for the simple financial life. But I'm here at my keyboard, yelling in print, because I know this system works. I have covered personal finance for, um, many, *many* years. I've watched fads come and go. I've seen trusting investors lose their money in bubbles while others made money the old-fashioned way. I've talked to the best people in the financial planning and investment worlds, and usually found that they manage their own money simply, too. I've tracked these rules of personal finance over decades, which is what gives me such confidence in them. One last thing I can promise: You'll find nothing in this book that I don't do myself.

These are my first rules:

Only a few things work, and they work really well.

If you set up a system that runs automatically, you can't fail.

Success comes from starting right, then keeping your itchy fingers off.

2. SPENDING AND SAVING

I'm Too Busy to Budget, Fuhgeddaboudit

No problem. You don't have to budget, or most of you don't. It takes too much time. It's picayune, boring, and a drag. When you're busy (heck, even when you're not), you don't want to bother adding up your bills week by week to see how you're doing.

I'm not saying budgets don't help. They're critical if you're living paycheck to paycheck, running up debt, and can't figure out why—about which, more later. Preparing a budget may also create an "aha!" moment, when you're amazed to see how much you're spending on fish tanks or gourmet beans. But right now, you want to get started—and without all that daily adding and subtracting that's such a pain. Life often interrupts that kind of budgeting. You lose receipts, your record-keeping crumbles, and you abandon the project.

So forget the classic budget for ordinary use. It's not even the real thing you need. You need what a budget achieves for you—namely, managing your spending so you can save more money for the rest of life (remember your list of goals?). Budgets are merely a tool for getting there.

I have a better idea: *automatic saving*. That does the basic budgeting for you, without the need to write down the coffee and doughnuts you buy in the morning or make imaginary spending plans (so much for "clothes," so much for "golf," so much for "veterinarian"—as if you could predict when your dog is going to need a hip replacement). It takes time and research to figure out how much you're likely to spend on each function, let alone having to juggle the books because you golfed too much this month. But adjusting your spending by saving money is as easy as rolling down a hill.

Before I explain, let me insert a short commercial for saving money. You'll never get anywhere if you're spending more than you earn. You'll have a great ride—vacations, furniture, cars, every possible new gadget. Your neighbors will think you're richer than they are, which I guess is the point. But the only chapter you'll need in this book is the one on managing debt. Any sudden change of life (serious illness, job interruption, divorce, forced retirement) will knock you down. Even if nothing major happens, you'll lie awake worrying about bills. Overspenders trust the Good Retirement Fairy to wave her wand and turn a meager 401(k) into a fortune. But the fairy retired and is living happily on her trust fund. On the success scale, steady saving wins.

THE SECRET OF SAVING MONEY, REVEALED

How do you save, given all the pressing expenses of daily life (fish tanks and so on)? Here's where the "simple" part comes in. You save by deliberately moving some money out of your checking account and into savings every month. Well, duh! But wait, there's more. When you have less in your checking account, you won't spend as much. You'll trim your expenses, here and there, without even thinking about it. It's *automatic budgeting*—as easy as that.

To get in the groove, arrange for a sum to be taken routinely from every paycheck, for savings and investments. You'll almost certainly spend all the rest of your pay, but your daily expenses will adjust themselves, magically, to the amount of money in your account. You will budget mentally, without having to write everything down.

Okay, I hear it. You're saying, "You're nuts. I can't save any more. I need my whole paycheck to pay my bills." Believe me, I understand the feeling. In fact, I've been there. That fear just happens to be wrong. There's always some money to spare, even in a paycheck-to-paycheck life. I can't explain it. All I know is that spending adjusts, up or down, for the amount of money available. By putting less cash at your fingertips, you're instantly ahead of the savings game.

I learned this in my twenties when I was a single working mother, struggling and not saving a dime. A friend advised me to sign up for the company retirement account and I said, "Not a chance, I can't afford it." He persisted until, with fear and trembling, I agreed to have 5 percent taken out of each paycheck and saved. What happened then? *Nothing* happened! I didn't consciously buy any less or get behind on my bills (or any more behind). My life didn't change, except that I started building my first little pot of savings. The hidden discipline of payroll deduction picked up the dollars that—even on my limited earnings—slipped through my fingers without a trace. I became a convert. Gradually, I raised my savings to 7 percent, then to 10 percent, before I felt a pinch. (That pinch kept me at 10 percent—for a while, at least.)

Why does automatic budgeting work? Beats me. Some quirk of mind lets you forget the money that's out of sight. You act as if what's in your checking account is all you have. Somehow, you offset your savings with little spending cuts that become part of your everyday household calculus. In a month, you'll find yourself living below your means without thinking about it. That's the only place savings can come from—the slice of your income you don't spend.

How much should you save? If you've picked up this book, you can easily save 5 percent of the money you earn. Despite student loans or dry-cleaning bills or rent or baby showers or gas for the car, you can save 5 percent. If you earn $40,000, that's $2,000 a year— roughly $38 a week or $5.50 a day. (Figure your savings on your gross pay, not your net after tax.) On earnings of $80,000, a 5 percent savings rate gives you $4,000 a year—roughly $77 a week or $11 a day. At $120,000, you'd save $6,000—$115 a week or $16.50 a day. If you feel that you're living on the edge, even these modest amounts may sound impossible. But remember, you're going to take this money out of your paycheck automatically. Your spending will shrink to fit.

In theory, of course, spending doesn't have to shrink. You could keep up your usual shopping (for a while, at least) and run up bigger credit-card bills. But oddly, people generally don't. We're all creatures of habit. If you normally limit your credit-card debt, you'll keep the same limit even when you're saving more. If you always pay in full each month, that pattern won't change. The magic of automatic saving spreads its aura, even over plastic. Sometimes debt bumps up a bit during the first or second month of a higher-savings regime, but your internal bean counting will soon bring it back to normal.

Saving 5 percent is just a toe-in-the-water start. Skip as fast as you can to saving 10 percent—an easy goal, even if you don't think so at first. Most people can save that much and not really notice. That's why 10 percent has been the eternal tithe. It's especially easy if you're contributing to a company 401(k) plan and your employer matches the money you put in. Your employer's contribution counts toward the 10 percent.

To retire well, however, you need to save more than 10 percent. The mutual fund company T. Rowe Price figures that, for a decent (not sterling) retirement, a 30-year-old with no savings should put

11 percent of earnings away. If you put off saving until you reach 40, you'd need to save 21 percent. That's a lot, even with an employer contribution—especially if you have kids to educate. The older you get, the harder reality bites. You can save more, but it takes a major adjustment in your standard of living. As you pass 50, you should at least be hoarding (not spending) the growing value of your house. That's a ready-made nest egg, to be tapped if your retirement income isn't as great as you'd hoped. Slow savers should add to their life plan a daily prayer for good health. To pay your bills, you'll probably need to work until 70 or later.

Early savings are worth more than later savings. Not that I'm knocking later savings—you need them, too. But the sooner money gets put away . . . well, you know the end of that sentence. What you may not know is how much that really means in cold, hard cash.

Take a look at the table on the next page—the tale of the Early Saver versus the Late Saver. Ms. Early puts away $1,000 a year at 5 percent for 15 years—$15,000 in all. After that, she quits saving and leaves her money alone to build. Mr. Late fritters away his money for 15 years, then gets religion and starts saving $1,000 a year, also at 5 percent. Forty years later, Mr. Late has deposited $40,000 but hasn't caught up with Ms. Early—*and never will!* Ms. Early will pull further ahead of him every year from now until the Third Millennium, even if she never saves another dime.

Why does this happen? Simple, old-fashioned compounding, nothing more. In Year 1, you earn interest on your savings, which fattens the size of your account. In Year 2, you earn interest on that larger amount, which fattens (or compounds) your savings again. In Year 3, you earn interest on that even larger amount, and so on and so on forever. Ms. Early's annual interest income grows so large that it stays well ahead of all Mr. Late's deposits. Time is money. You can read it on the next page.

HOW THE EARLY SAVER BEATS THE LATE SAVER

I wish I could give this chart to every young (and youngish) person walking down the street. It applies not only to cash savings but also to investments in a retirement account. The earlier money goes in, the more it can earn for you.

	Early Saver	Late Saver
	Deposits $1,000 a year at 5%	Deposits Nothing
Year 1	$1,051	$0
Year 5	5,824	0
Year 10	13,301	0
Year 15	22,903	0
	Stops depositing	Deposits $1,000 a year at 5%
Year 16	$24,077	$1,051
Year 20	29,407	5,824
Year 25	37,758	13,301
Year 30	48,482	22,903
Year 35	62,251	35,230
Year 40	79,931	51,060
Year 45	102,631	71,384
Year 50	131,779	97,482
Year 55	169,205	130,990

SOURCE: Richard L. D. Morse

A LITTLE BIT OF BUDGETING

Once you push your savings above 10 percent, you'll probably have to make some deliberate choices. Some of you still will be able to budget in your heads, even while saving 15 percent of your savings and more. Others will need a spending plan to work out your priorities. You'll definitely need a plan if you're running on credit cards and hope. You also should make a plan if your income drops—say, you're quitting a job or getting divorced—or if you see big expenses ahead. You need a peek at what you can and can't afford.

I warn you that real budgeting involves homework. You have to find out what you're spending now (you only think you know). When you add everything up, you'll be surprised at how much you lavish on family favorites—clothes, eating out, entertainments, gadgets, gardening, whatever. There's no need to cut all these things out. You'll simply find cheaper substitutes, once you've raised saving and investing to a higher spot on your priority list.

Often, just making the plan is enough. Once you've examined your spending, you'll know exactly where and how much to cut. Raise your automatic savings by that amount, to supply the discipline.

To make a formal plan, dig out the records of what you spent in the past six months—your check registers, bank statements, and credit-card statements (you keep them, I hope). It's even better to look at a year's worth of spending, but six months will do. Break your expenses into categories, such as "mortgage," "electric," "school tax," "life insurance," "gasoline," "gifts," and so on. Be specific. Instead of "clothes," list "his clothes," "her clothes," and "kid's clothes." (You know how to do this. I don't have to go on.)

While you're listing expenses, use a marking system to help find possible spending cuts. Put an E next to essential items, such as mortgage or rent. Put an F (for fun) next to things you don't need but that seem basic to your happiness. Put an X next to purchases that, on reflection, you could have lived without. Couples should work on this list together (the Xs may be the hardest part). You'll be surprised at how big the X number is (the food dehydrator? the sixteenth pair of sexy shoes? the Acura instead of the Honda?). That's the kind of spending to dump—intentionally, if you're making a plan, and instinctively, if you're managing your money by ear. On the Fun list, look for substitutes. You like to eat out with friends, but could you have them over for spaghetti instead? Could you and your siblings agree to quit exchanging holiday gifts? As for your Essentials list, it's not as immutable as it looks. You can refinance your mortgage, buy cheaper life insurance, or turn down the thermostats.

You should also spend a couple of weeks tracking the cash you walk around with, especially the credit cards that walk around with you. Plenty is written about the "latte factor." If you're paying $3 every day for expensive coffee to drink at work, and cut it out, you'll save $780 a year toward a retirement plan. But c'mon, cheap coffee costs $1.50, so you've really saved only $390 while hating it every minute.

The latte factor isn't your problem. The question is, what shops do you pass to and from the coffee shop? Do you walk to a bus or subway and see the perfect pink handbag in a store window? Do you steer your car toward an electronics shop for a bit of gear? Whether you go to a workplace or not, what else are you buying while you're running personal or household errands? Male or female, you can find your eye lighting on a dozen spending ideas. Stores, catalogs, online shopping sites, TV shopping, everything tempts. That's what to track over a month, including the cost of eating out, ordering in, and buying food you never use. Everyone can get a little sloppy with cash and it's smart to notice. But what's squeezing you is the big stuff that you ladle onto your credit card. Try raising your annual saving by the amount of money on your X list. That won't limit your style: it will simply, and profitably, limit the things it occurs to you to buy.

You can probably stop there. You're now saving more money and know which shop windows to avoid.

For a more formal plan, you have to put written caps on your spending, keep your receipts, and check every couple of weeks to see if you stuck to the rule. That's even more homework, and some people learn to love it. If you hate it, however, it needn't last very long. Once you've recognized the black holes in your spending and made a serious effort to plug them, you'll get used to the change without tracking the dollars all the time.

Now for the hard cases—people drowning in debt and deep in denial about their financial lives. They're saving little or nothing but can't jump off the bobsled they're riding downhill. Typical stories are couples in their thirties or forties who make a good living but spend it on status. Their house is too big, their mortgage too high, their vacations too ritzy, their credit cards too stretched, and they can't understand why it's so hard to live on what they're making. Or maybe you're single, living high while struggling with big student loans. To dig yourself out of a hole like this takes some serious self-examination. If you've tried and failed to reorient your life, turn to a financial planner—not one who sells financial products on commission, but a planner who charges only fees for his or her time. (For more on planners, see Chapter 8.)

When a planner enters your life, your homework balloons. You'll have to track every nickel of spending, confess to the size of your debt, compare your bills with your monthly income, and tote up the value of your investments (including those doggy stocks you're so very sorry you bought). The planner will crunch the numbers to show you the meager retirement you face unless you make a change, and where your excess spending lies.

Reordering your priorities goes well beyond budgets. Now we're talking life change for people who haven't been able to face the facts—downsizing to a smaller house, budgeting for health insurance, giving up on private schools. Most of you aren't in this sort of pickle. But when you are and can't fix it yourself, the right planner is your fastest route to financial health.

FAST AND EASY FINANCIAL TRACKING

Some people budget the old-fashioned way, by putting a fixed amount of cash into envelopes marked "groceries," "gas," and "vacation fund." Others use budget books and spreadsheets bought at an office-supply store—devoting one column to "planned expenses," another to "actual expenses," and a third to "oops." But you can chop the paperwork by going electronic.

Start with online banking. Fifty-three million people—one-fourth of all adults—now bank online. You should be among them if you own a computer, if your bank offers the service (most do), and if you have more than a handful of bills each month. My computer-allergic husband used to handwrite checks to pay the bills. When he died and I took over the job, I hated the hours it took to write and stamp and mail, let alone keep track of the balance in the check register (ugh). So I called my bank, signed up for free online banking and bill-paying, and breathed "whew."

I'm not a computer adept, so trust me when I say that online bill-paying isn't hard to learn. To set up your system, you simply enter the names and addresses of the various places you buy from (it helps to have someone read them to you while you type; it also helps to have your brother do it for you). Now I pay bills every couple of weeks. Click on my bank account, click click click on the names of the people and stores I owe money to, fill in the amounts, click OK, and off they go. Your payees don't need online accounts themselves. The bank simply mails them a check. I still write a few checks by hand, but only to people I don't expect to have to pay again. You can also receive bills through your online account; several hundred companies stand ready to send them electronically, if asked. You view your bills and pay them whenever you want.

Something else I like about online banking—it ends your struggle with your checkbook. Click, your current balance shows. Click, you see the cash you withdrew from the ATM. Click, you get a list of the people you've paid and the checks that haven't been cashed. Click, you see the remaining balance after you've paid your latest bills. Click, you transfer money from savings to checking and back again. Click, you set up or cancel automatic payments to cover your regular bills—mortgage, insurance premium, car lease, utilities. Click, you see that your paycheck arrived (most employers will deposit it electronically).

If you haven't tried online banking, you'll be amazed at the time you save. You'll pay your bills, then toss off a few games of solitaire before moving on. Best of all, there's no need to balance your checkbook any more or, if you didn't anyway, no need to keep checking balances by phone or at the ATM. All ATM withdrawals show up automatically, so you can't forget them. I do keep a written tally of the few checks I write by hand, so I know how much remains outstanding and can subtract it from the balance that shows online. You might want to keep a similar tally of debit-card transactions; sometimes it takes them a while to hit your account.

What about security? Some of you avoid online banking because you're afraid that hackers will reach through cyberspace and steal your money or your identity. I have good news and bad news. The bad news is that big-time thieves usually steal identities wholesale, not retail. That is, they attack the central computer where stores and other companies keep their customer records, rather than try to decode individual passwords. You're vulnerable to ID theft whether you bank online or not, so you might as well do it. Banking sites are among the most secure, and that's the good news. If someone steals money directly from your account—say, by lifting your ATM card and PIN—the bank is responsible, just as it would be for a forged check. You'd have to persuade the bank that the culprit wasn't your teenager or spendthrift spouse. But, again, this could happen whether or not you use an online bank account. The bank will definitely pay if its own security is breached.

Smaller banks and credit unions may not offer online accounts. For bill-paying, you can turn to companies such as CheckFree (a free service) or PayTrust (for about $5 or $13 a month, depending on the package you choose).

To budget electronically, get one of the two leading financial programs, Quicken or Microsoft Money. These take more time to learn, so they're recommended only for people who love to cuddle with their computers. The initial setup isn't a walk in the park. But once everything works, you'll have a budget spreadsheet on-screen, listing all the usual categories ("mortgage," "clothes," "restaurants," and so on). Some of your spending has to be entered by hand. Some can be downloaded automatically from your accounts at major banks and credit-card companies. When you have up-to-date records, you just click to compare your actual spending with what you budgeted. Click, to see what you spent in various categories. Click, to show all your tax-deductible expenses. Click, to project next year's spending and saving compared with next year's expected take-home pay. To make these programs useful, however, you have to keep them current—and busy people may not have the time.

If computers aren't your game, then it's paper-and-pencil for budgets and write-and-stamp for bills. You still don't have to balance your checkbook exactly; the bank computers can add and subtract well enough. But at least keep a running tally of how much is left in your account. Banks charge $25 to $35 if you bounce a check. What's more, the person who got your bad check might have to pay his or her bank a $25 handling fee. You'll be expected to make good on that as well.

SOMETHING IMPORTANT THAT EVERYONE SHOULD SAVE FOR

Remember your list of goals? There's one you probably forgot to mention: building what I call a Cushion Fund. These funds are often referred to as "emergency savings"—a name I don't like. No one expects emergencies so they don't bother to prepare. Cushion Funds are something else. They add a layer of security to your life, for unexpected (not "emergency") expenses. If you or someone in your family has health problems, you need an even larger Cushion Fund, to help cover medical costs that aren't insured.

Holding cash in a Cushion Fund may go against the grain, especially when interest rates are low. You think, "I'm not an elephant, why should I store up a thousand dollars in a bank account that's paying peanuts?" But forget the interest rate. This money isn't an investment, it's part of your financial and emotional safety net. You won't be as stressed about sudden expenses when you know you have cash available, just in case. Cushion Funds won't make you rich, but they can save you from becoming poor.

How much money should you put aside? Aim for three times your basic monthly expenses (mortgage or rent, groceries, car payment, gasoline, phone, utilities, insurance, minimum credit-card payments, health insurance). If you're self-employed and paychecks arrive irregularly, stashing five or six times expenses would be more prudent.

Don't mix your Cushion Fund with money you're saving for special purposes, such as vacations and holiday gifts. It's too easy to spend the whole amount, cushion and all. It might cost you a little more to keep two savings accounts instead of one, but it's worth it if it helps you keep your fingers off. Build up your cushion with automatic deposits from your checking account, plus any bonuses and cash gifts you get. For your own security, you want to grow this account as fast as you can. Once you've reached your savings goal, don't even look at the totals when the monthly statements arrive— you're pretending the money isn't there. If you have to tap the account, refill it as fast as you can.

Where should you keep your Cushion Fund? Three months' expenses should be stored right at hand, in the safest possible place. For small balances, use a bank savings account. For balances of $1,000 to $3,000, you have two choices:

1. *A bank money-market deposit account*—easy to start, just ask your bank to open it up. Interest rates change from time to time (whenever the bank decides) and the accounts are federally insured. You're normally limited to six transfers or withdrawals a month, three of which can be by check or debit card. If that's not enough, you can transfer money to your regular checking account.

2. *A money-market mutual fund*—also easy to start, especially if you own other mutual funds. Go to the fund group you're using now and simply add a money fund to your account. It works much like a bank account. You deposit cash, earn interest, and can withdraw your savings at any time. Money funds are considered safe, even though they aren't federally insured (they've never lost a cent for individuals). Interest rates change daily, in line with rates in the open market. Usually (but not always), money-fund rates run just a bit higher than the rates offered by banks. You can write an unlimited number of checks on your fund, typically in amounts of $250 or $500 and up.

Choose whichever type of cushion-fund account is most convenient. Personally, I use a tax-free money-market mutual fund, which yields a slightly higher return for people in the 25 percent tax bracket and up. Also, my money fund isn't right under my nose all the time, the way my bank account is, so I'm less tempted to spend the cash.

For savings that exceed three months' expenses, consider a higher-rate investment:

1. *The bank option:* A three-month or six-month certificate of deposit. You tie up your money for that short period of time, in return for a slightly higher rate of interest. Keep reinvesting, every time the CD comes due. You pay a small penalty if you have to withdraw your money before the CD matures, but that probably won't happen.

2. *The mutual-fund option:* A short-term bond fund that invests in bonds maturing in three years or less. You can sell at any time. The market value of shares in a bond mutual fund will rise and fall as interest rates change; in a poor market, you could lose a little money. Still, short-term bond funds don't carry a lot of risk. They're an acceptable bet for money that you hope, with luck, you won't have to touch.

3. *The combination Cushion Fund—a super choice:* Open a Roth IRA retirement plan (see page 32) and store your cushion savings in the plan's money-market mutual fund. If you need some cash, you can take it out at any time, without penalty. If you never need the cash, your interest earnings grow tax-free.

HOW MUCH SHOULD YOU SAVE FOR YOUR RETIREMENT?

How about saving *lots*? You'll have Social Security in some form, which is worth a great deal. If you work for an old-line company, you might have a pension (although pension plans are on their way out). If you have a 401(k), your employer might contribute.

But mostly, you'll retire only with what you save and invest yourself.

It takes large amounts of money to live well without a paycheck coming in. The sooner you start saving, the more you'll have and the gladder you will be. Whenever I've interviewed people approaching or in retirement and asked what, if anything, they wish they had done differently, they always say, "I wish I had saved more money." Now that you know, you can fulfill that future wish today.

In general, you should be saving at least 10 percent of your income if you're in your mid-twenties and 15 percent if you're in your mid-thirties and haven't started saving yet. By your forties, nonsavers would have to save at least 25 percent—probably not possible, especially if you have kids (you'll simply have to revise your retirement plans). These savings percentages include whatever your employer might contribute to your 401(k), so workers with a company match plan are way ahead. You lose your advantage, however, if you take out the money and spend it when you switch jobs.

To get more specific about how much you ought to save each month, based on your current earnings and savings, I recommend strongly that you fill in a retirement income calculator. Pencil-and-paper people can use the Ballpark Estimate, produced by the Employee Benefit Research Institute and Research Fund and reproduced in the Appendix. You'll find a more sophisticated version online at Choosetosave.org. For other good calculators, check Dinkytown.net, Troweprice.com, and Vanguard.com.

The sites won't agree exactly, because their methods are different. But all of them give you a reasonable target to shoot for. If the target shocks you because it's more than you think you can save, don't turn away. These numbers are telling you the truth. If you save less, you're "planning" for a diminished standard of living in your later years (or dreaming of a miracle).

PUTTING YOUR WHOLE FINANCIAL LIFE ON CRUISE CONTROL

Automatic payments help with more than just your budgeting. Once you learn to trust them, they can order your life in many useful ways. They're the path to your objective: a simple financial setup that leaves you free to focus on the more interesting things you do. Automatic management also fosters financial moderation— a virtue in itself. Your apparently "rich" neighbors, whose every paycheck and bonus fly out the window, will have to retire to a cheaper digs in their later years, out of touch with their former friends, and struggling to get by. You'll ask, "Where are the Joneses everybody tried to keep up with?" Where indeed.

Once you start planning, you'll find many great ways of automating and redirecting your spending and savings.

First Automatic Savings Idea: An Employer Retirement Plan

Sign up for your employer's plan—a 401(k), 403(b), 457, federal Thrift Savings Plan, or whatever. A percentage of your pay (you name the amount) will be diverted into a personal retirement account, usually invested in mutual funds. From the very start, these accounts put you two big steps ahead. First, there's no income or Social Security tax on your contribution, so you're investing money that otherwise would go to the government. Second, most employers match at least part of the money you put up. If you put in $1,000, your employer might add $500 or even another $1,000 to your account. That's like finding a stack of free money in the street. Be sure to contribute as least enough to get every dollar that the company will pay. Otherwise, you're pocketing only part of that stack of money and throwing the rest away. (If you aren't sure how much you need to contribute to get the maximum match, ask the employee benefits department. You yourself can contribute anywhere up to $15,000 in 2006, plus an extra $5,000 if you're 50 or older.)

A few companies let you sign up for automatic annual increases in your contribution, often tied to the month you might expect a raise. Always say yes. You might forget to increase your contributions yourself, or avoid even thinking about it. You can stop the automatic increases if you change your mind, but don't. You won't notice them and you'll be fattening your retirement fund.

401(k)s and 403(b)s come in two types:

- A *traditional plan*, where your contribution is tax-deductible. Until 2006, all plans were traditional, so that's what almost everyone has. You pay taxes on the money when you take it out.
- A *Roth plan*, with no tax deduction for contributions. Instead, all your earnings build tax-free. If you choose the Roth, your taxes will be higher in the current year. Your reward is peace of mind. You won't care if tax rates rise in the future because you can take money out of your Roth with nary a dime of taxes due. There's another plus: When you leave the company, you can roll your money directly into a Roth IRA, which gives you more flexibility than you get from a regular IRA (page 31). Roths aren't widely available yet; employers were first allowed to offer them starting in January 2006. But they'll grow.

Stretch to put away as much money as you can (make it 5 percent more than you originally intended). If you're wavering, think about the Early Saver. These are the best years of your retirement-savings life. Start investing even with only 3 percent of pay. You cannot imagine what a difference this will make, when you're 60 and looking back. If you say, "I'll join the plan later," you may never get around to it. You'll become a Late Saver and never catch up.

The usual time for joining a retirement plan is when you're

hired. You get an enrollment form, asking how much to take from your paycheck and where to invest it. Don't be put off because you don't know how to choose among the plan's many mutual funds. It's easy. See Chapter 7. If you never got around to joining, call the employee benefits department and sign up right now. Time is money, time's passing, this is your time.

If you're already in a plan, raise the amount you're contributing. Maybe you think you can't afford it, but taking the long view, you can't afford not to. I don't care if your buddies tell you not to bother investing because the plan isn't very good (any payroll-deduction saving is good). I don't care if your company doesn't match your contribution (these are still pretax dollars, so you're investing with some of the government's money). Take this easy way of paying yourself first.

One more thing: If you leave the job and get a payout from the plan, don't spend it, even if the amount seems too small to matter. If you do, you'll throw away everything you gained from early saving—your contribution, the company match, and all of the account's future, tax-deferred, compounded value. You'll also owe taxes on that money, plus a 10 percent penalty on the earnings for withdrawing them before you reached age 59½.

Instead, keep your savings growing by rolling them into an Individual Retirement Account at a mutual-fund company. For suggestions, see Chapter 7. The fund company will handle it for you. A $3,500 payout rolled into an IRA and invested in mutual funds earning 8 percent a year will be worth $16,315 in 20 years and $35,220 in 30 years, without your lifting a finger. A $10,000 payout will grow to $46,610 in 20 years and $100,630 in 30 years. *That's* compounding. With good luck and good markets, you'll earn even more.

Second Automatic Savings Idea:
A Personal Retirement Plan You Start Yourself

You gotta do it, especially when you have no employer plan. You want to keep the wolf out in the woods when you're old and gray, not at your door. There are plenty of personal plans to choose from. Contributions are tax-deductible and the earnings tax-deferred, so you're still investing with money you'd otherwise owe the government.

Retirement plans are easy to start. Just call your bank or a mutual-fund company such as Fidelity (800-343-3548), T. Rowe Price (800-225-5132), or Vanguard (877-662-7447), or visit their websites and get the sign-up form. Fill it in, pick the mutual funds you want for your retirement investments (again, see Chapter 7 for my favorites), send in a check, and you're done. To grow your savings without any further thought, arrange for a monthly check to go from your bank account to your retirement account automatically. You can set up the payment yourself, via online banking, or ask the bank to make the transfer (the fund company will tell you how). Time the payments to coincide with the day your paycheck clears. If you're paid biweekly, take your rent or mortgage from one of the checks you get each month and your retirement-savings contribution from the other. You can change these payments at any time.

As usual, the key to success is *automate!* You can promise yourself that you'll write a regular check to your retirement account, but over time, you won't. You'll use a little of the money for this, and then a little more for that, and next thing you know you're saving only half of what you intended, or less. The funny thing is, you'll convince yourself that you're still on track if you're writing any check at all. Financial self-deception can continue for years. There's just one sure way of staying right with your money: Set up a simple system, let it run by itself, and keep out of the way.

Automatic saving becomes a little more complicated for people who are self-employed. If you can count on a sizable regular payment each month, take some or all of your savings contribution out of that. For safety, add "reserve checking" to your bank account. That gives you a credit line to back up your contribution, just in case your client pays late. When the client's money finally arrives, repay the reserve account immediately. If all your income arrives irregularly, however, don't automate unless you can keep a large cushion in your account. Alternatively, write your retirement account a check for 10 percent (or more) of every payment you receive. No cheating! The first time you shave a deposit, you're lost. Continuous contributions work better than funding your retirement account at the end of the year, from whatever money is left. There is never anything left.

Here are the leading individual retirement plans.

- *A traditional Individual Retirement Account, for people not covered by company plans.* You can deposit up to $4,000 a year ($5,000 if you're 50 and older) and deduct it on your tax return. Starting in 2008, you'll be allowed to contribute even more. Mutual funds typically require $1,000 or $2,000 to open an IRA, although a few will start with as little as $50 a month if it's deposited automatically. Any money withdrawn is taxed. There's normally a 10 percent penalty on IRA earnings taken before age 59½. Starting at 70½, regular withdrawals are required. For all the details on IRAs, including important information on how to maintain the tax shelter when leaving money to heirs, get the valuable book *Parlay Your IRA into a Family Fortune* by Ed Slott.
- *A SEP-IRA for the self-employed.* A SEP is a traditional IRA fashioned as a Simplified Employee Pension. You can contribute and deduct as much as 25 percent of your gross income, up to a maximum contribution of $44,000 in 2006 (that limit is adjusted for inflation every year). There's no extra paperwork

with SEP-IRAs after the sign-up. You report the deduction on your personal tax return.

- *An individual 401(k) for the self-employed.* Use this plan if you're flush. You can probably put away more than a SEP-IRA would allow. Right out of the box, you can save up to $15,000 of your earnings in 2006, with no restrictions. If $15,000 is all you earn, you could save every dime (assuming, of course, that someone else is paying your bills). If you're 50 and up, you can throw in another $5,000. In addition, you can add as much as 25 percent of your earnings, up to a combined maximum contribution of $44,000 if you're under 50 and $49,000 if you're older.

- *Roth IRAs for both short-term and retirement savings.* Anyone with earnings—both employees and the self-employed—can start a Roth. The only requirement is that your paycheck fall within the income limits. You're allowed to deposit up to $4,000 a year in after-tax money ($5,000 if you're 50 and older). All of your investment earnings—interest, dividends, and capital gains—will grow entirely tax-free as long as you leave them in the Roth until you reach 59½ and have held the account for at least five years. After that, you can do whatever you want with the money—take some or all of it out, or leave it for your heirs. You get the full Roth contribution if you earn up to $95,000 a year ($150,000 for married couples). If you earn more, the amount you're allowed to contribute declines, phasing out at $110,000 for singles and $160,000 for couples.

Here's the special beauty of a Roth: Unlike other retirement plans, it doesn't lock your savings up. You can withdraw the money you contributed at any time, and for any reason, without owing taxes and penalties. For example, say you've invested $8,000 over two years and earned $650 on your money. Then you lose your job, run through your Cushion Fund (you have one, right?), and still need cash. Or maybe you decide to buy a second home. You can raid your Roth for your original

$8,000, no matter how old you are or how long you've had the account. Only your earnings ($650 in this example) have to stay in the account for the required length of time. So a Roth does double duty: It's a tax-favored, long-term retirement fund that also can function as a Cushion Fund.

You might use a Roth if the choices are poor in your company 401(k). Put just enough in the 401(k) to capture the employer match, then use the Roth for the rest of your retirement investment.

If you have a choice, should you use a traditional IRA or a Roth? You can't compare the financial results; they'll depend on your tax bracket when you retire. So consider two things. (1) *What you can afford*. Traditional IRAs cost less upfront, thanks to the tax deduction for contributions. (2) *Flexibility*. Roth IRAs let you leave the money untouched past 70½—a good choice, if you'll have plenty of other assets to live on. With Roths, you can also withdraw your contributions at any time, leaving you better prepared for whatever life throws at you. For lots more detail on Roths and traditional IRAs, see Rothira.com.

• *Rollover IRAs for people leaving employee retirement plans and receiving lump-sum payouts*. Please don't spend the lump-sum payout you receive. Keep the tax shelter intact by shifting your money directly into a traditional IRA, if you're leaving a plain-vanilla employer plan, or a Roth IRA if your plan was a Roth. Rollover IRAs can accept any amount of money, in a bulk transfer, regardless of how much you earn. If you already have the appropriate IRA, the payout can be rolled right into it.

Third Automatic Savings Idea: Pay Off Your Credit-Card Debt

Maybe you didn't think of repaying debt as saving money, but think again. You're saving the future annual interest you'd otherwise pay, which puts cash directly into your pocket. Every dollar used to reduce your credit-card debt earns a return that equals the card's interest rate. For example, paying down a 12 percent debt gives you a 12 percent yield on your money, guaranteed. Paying down a 20 percent debt gives you a 20 percent return. That's the highest safe return the market offers. So set up a speedy debt-repayment plan, even if it squeezes your style for a little while (didn't you always know this day would come?). The more you pay, the less interest you're charged and the faster your debt will drop. How to repay? You guessed it—automatically, from your checking account.

Fourth Automatic Savings Idea: Reinvest All Dividends

Next to gravity and the tides, compounding is nature's strongest force. And I mean *strong*. An investor who put $100 into Standard & Poor's 500-stock average on the last day of 1925, held it until the last day of 2004, and reinvested all the dividends, would have earned a huge $253,220, according to a calculation by Ibbotson Associates. If that same investor had taken out all the dividends and spent them, the gain would have come to a measly $9,400. Hard to believe, but true. That's the power of compounding.

When you own a mutual fund, you can reinvest all dividends in new fund shares automatically. Your gains compound without any effort on your part. By contrast, if you own individual stocks that pay dividends, you might have to take the money in cash. That makes it easy to fritter away. (Some companies offer shareholders a dividend reinvestment plan. For more information on these plans, see Dripcentral.com.)

Fifth Automatic Savings Idea: Start a College Fund

Every state runs tax-deferred college savings plans. You'll find the details in Chapter 6. I mention them here because all these plans love automatic contributions. Depending on your state, you can start with as little as $50 a month.

Sixth Automatic Savings Idea: Pay Off Your Mortgage

Your home is your piggy bank, or ought to be. As you pay off the mortgage, more of the value of the house becomes yours to keep. There's nothing so sweet as a paid-up home when you finally move from full-time work into your retirement years.

At the moment, that sounds like a dinosaur of an idea. Homes feel more like ATMs. Owners are stripping the value out, by taking home-equity loans or doing cash-out refinancings (you "cash out" when you take a new and larger mortgage, pay off the older, smaller loan, and pocket the difference). Some of you are using that money to make financial investments—stocks, annuities, insurance policies, anything that sounds good in a salesperson's mouth.

That won't simplify your life. Instead, it adds a lot of risk. If your investments lose value, you'll have wasted your home equity and will be stuck with the misery of higher mortgage payments, besides.

You might tap your home equity for a down payment on a second home. That works, as long as you're sure you can cover both mortgages every month. When you're a two-home owner, you should keep extra savings in the bank, just in case your income drops. You want to be sure you can pay all your bills, if you have to sell one of the houses and it takes a while.

Homeowners have more financial freedom when they let their home equity build. It serves as a second Cushion Fund and saves you from mortgage debt when you're not working anymore.

Your bank will cheerfully automate your mortgage payments, or you can set up the payments yourself through your online account. But why stop there? Add an extra $100 or $200 a month, to reduce the principal of the loan. Every extra payment lowers the future amount of interest you have to pay. It also adds to your equity, meaning more cash in hand whenever you sell.

SHE'S CRAZY, I CAN'T DO ALL THIS

You're shaking your head. I've proposed so many automated payments that you feel broke. But this system is truly more affordable than you think. You'd be paying the mortgage and the credit cards anyway. Raising your retirement contributions won't pinch your standard of living (try it; you'll see!). The Cushion Fund might be a stretch, at first, but it's basic to a No Worry financial life. How do you put all these pieces together? Here's how the priorities run:

1. For retirement, you *must* put 10 percent or 15 percent away. Start with 10 percent, if you haven't yet taken care of the two other "musts" on this list. After that, go to 15 percent or more (include any employer contributions in your count).
2. You *must* reduce, then eliminate, credit-card debt. Paying consumer interest is like feeding your money to the squirrels.
3. You *must* create a Cushion Fund. If you're still battling credit-card debt, start with a cushion just large enough to cover your expenses for a single month. Turn the rest of your budgeting toward a debt repayment plan. If you've already saved more than one month's expenses, use the extra to pay down your credit cards—that's the smartest use of the money. Once your cards are clean, you can redirect your monthly payments toward building, or rebuilding, your cushion account.
4. If you have kids and expect to help with their higher education, college savings come next. These plans are an option, however, not a must. It's an error to put college ahead of retirement savings, if you can't afford both. Kids can always get student loans that give them 10 years or more to repay. But banks don't make

retirement loans. Your kids will thank you, if you're able get through your later years without their help.

5. Prepaying your mortgage comes last. Stick to your regular payment schedule while you're taking care of the items higher on this list. Once you've adjusted to your new, automatic-savings regime, I predict that you'll find a way to add to your mortgage payments, too.

SO HERE ARE YOUR OPTIONS

Save nothing, live like a king today but on a pittance (or on your kids) when you retire.

Save something, live like a prince today but with only minimal comforts when you retire.

Save lots and live well—both now and when you retire.

Looked at that way, what's to choose?

3. WIPE OUT YOUR DEBT

Financial Ecology: Use Your Money, Don't Throw It Away

Would you set fire to a stack of $100 bills? Would you wash your windows with $20s, ball them up, and throw them away? Naturally not, dumb of me to ask. So why would you carry debt on your credit cards? You're throwing away your money on interest payments every month. Even if you shift the debt to a lower-interest home-equity loan, you've still got that hole in your wallet. Waste is waste.

If you're debt-free already, congratulations—you get a free pass to Chapter 4. Otherwise, hang around. Your next step toward an easy, automated financial life is creating a system for zeroing out your consumer loans.

To start, you have to wrap your mind around the exact amount you owe. Go back to the list you made for Chapter 1—you know, that list of debts that you never added up. Add, please. You can set aside your mortgage and auto loans—they're usually not optional. What you need to dump is consumer debt, including credit cards, home-equity loans, and installment loans. How much are you paying every month (more than the minimum, I hope)? What's the interest rate? Are your credit-card balances going down or up? Once you go through this exercise, you'll probably find that the totals aren't bad at all, compared with your income. You *can* repay, it has simply been easier not to.

Now I'm writing in a whisper: If you're married, does your wife or husband know the truth? Spouses who keep separate bank and credit-card accounts may also keep financial secrets, including a pile of hidden debt. Even when you have joint accounts, the spouse who always pays the bills could get away with splurges the other hasn't noticed. A splurger dreams of finding the money to repay without ever having to confess—and that's possible, if each of you institutes a separate debt reduction plan. But I vote for confession. It's one thing to bury a small extravagance in the daily bill, but quite another to burden the marriage with a large and dark expense. It's equally wrong to hide some of your income or bully your spouse about every personal bill. Whatever your financial crimes, put them on the table, beg for a suspended sentence, and work toward a single future as a team.

Here's your simple, four-part program for getting out of debt: Throw some cash at the problem. Cut the interest rates you pay. Set up fixed, automated monthly repayments on each debt. Finally, live on your income, without falling into debt again (easy—you'll see). Now for the details . . .

FIRST DEBT-BEATER: THROW CASH AT THE PROBLEM

Shake loose some spare money for instant reductions in your loan balances. Possibilities include year-end bonuses, dividend checks, birthday gifts, proceeds from a yard sale, and other little showers of cash. Next, tap any savings you have in the bank. It's pointless to hoard a bank account earning, say, 3 percent while paying 16 percent on your debts. You're losing 13 percent a year on that deal. Keep just one month's basic living expenses in the bank, in case something unexpected happens, and use the rest of your savings to pay down your credit cards.

It may also pay to raise cash by selling shares of stocks or mutual funds, if they're not in a tax-deferred retirement plan. When they're worth less than you paid, you can write off the loss on your tax return and use the proceeds to cut your debt. When they're worth more, you'll owe a tax on the gain, but that might not matter if the gain, and the tax, are small.

You might think it's smarter to keep your investments, because they'll grow. But they're unlikely to grow fast enough to make up for the money you're losing by paying credit-card interest. You get a better return on your money by paying off the debt.

I'll explain that with an example. Say you sold $5,000 worth of mutual fund shares and used the proceeds to wipe out a $5,000 debt. The debt was costing you 16 percent per year in interest charges, so repaying it saves you 16 percent—not just this year, but for every year in the future that the debt would have lasted. If you kept the shares, they'd have had to earn 16 percent just to cover the cost of the interest you're paying, and more than 16 percent for you to make any money. No stock or mutual fund in the world can guarantee you a 16 percent return. If you're paying 20 percent interest, the stock has to earn 20 percent for you to break even, financially.

Remember: Every dollar you use to reduce a debt gives you an investment return equal to the debt's interest rate, guaranteed. Credit-card interest rates are always high, so reducing this debt yields a high return on your money. Pay down your highest-rate debts first, then move to your cheaper ones. When you're clean, use automatic savings to build up your investments again.

SECOND DEBT-BEATER: CUT THE INTEREST RATES YOU CURRENTLY PAY

There are three ways:

1. *Call each of your credit-card companies and ask for a lower rate on your unpaid balances*—if not permanently, then at least for six months or a year. Tell the bank's phone representative that your card isn't competitive. Read the phone rep any low-rate offer you recently got in the mail or found on the Web. Stay friendly, keep chatting, say that, without a rate cut, you'll switch to the better card. If the rep holds firm, remind him or her that, after you switch, the bank will almost certainly mail you a cut-rate offer. There's a fifty-fifty chance the rep will finally say okay. If not, hang up and try another rep. If you're still stonewalled, carry through on your threat to switch.

2. *Switch to a cheaper credit card.* If your credit is good, you can usually get a zero (or low) interest rate for the first 6 to 12 months. But check the terms carefully, to see what the zero interest covers. Credit-card companies always have tricks up their sleeves. Unless you're alert, you'll wind up paying more interest than you expected (and maybe not even saving money!).

   A typical offer gives you a zero rate—but only on balances transferred from other cards. That sounds like a good deal. So you get the card and start to use it for new purchases. *Then* you discover the trick. The card company doesn't let you pay off those new purchases—at least not right away. When you send in a payment, every dollar will be applied to your zero-rate debt. Your new charges will be treated as unpaid balances, on which you have to pay the regular interest rate.

   For example, say you accept a card with a regular rate of 16 percent on unpaid balances but a promotional zero-interest rate on balances transferred from another card. You transfer $8,000 and use your new card to make $400 in purchases. When your first bill comes, you send a $600 payment, intending to cover the $400 in new charges and chop $200 off your debt. Sorry, no such luck. The card company will apply the entire $600 to the zero-interest debt. Your new purchases become an unpaid balance, costing you 16 percent. Every future payment is handled the same way until the zero-rate balance is gone or your so-called free period ends. Meanwhile, the cost of carrying your new purchases compounds.

Once you know the game, it's easy to beat. Don't use the "bargain" card for new purchases as long as the special, zero-interest period lasts. Set up automatic repayments to wipe out as much of this debt as you can (you can reduce it faster when you're not paying high interest rates). Shop only with your older cards, paying those bills in full each month. Start using the new card after the bargain-interest period has passed.

You won't have this problem if the zero-rate offer covers new purchases as well as your transferred balances. So always check.

Another trick is to charge zero interest on transferred balances but impose a fee for the transfer. That undercuts your savings. If you're transferring balances from several cards, a fee will apply to each transfer.

Some zero-rate deals cover only new purchases, not transferred balances. If you don't notice that little wrinkle and transfer a balance anyway, you'll pay the full interest rate on that debt, plus a transfer fee.

One more warning—be sure to make every payment on time, not only on your new card but on all your other credit cards and debts. One late payment and bang—you'll be jumped to the regular rate (read all about it in the fine print). A second late payment may kick you up to a penalty rate of 25 percent, 30 percent, or even more. There's also a late charge as high as $40 a pop. How will the card company discover that you paid another debt late? By running regular checks on your credit history (see page 49). Once you put your debt repayments on autopilot, however, you'll never miss.

3. *Pay off your high-rate credit cards with a lower-rate loan against your house.* There are three ways of doing this:

You can refinance your mortgage. Borrow more than you need to repay the old mortgage and use the extra money to wipe out consumer debt. This makes sense if the interest rate on your new loan will be lower than the rate on the loan you have now. You're getting a twofer—a cheaper mortgage as well as a cut in the rate on your credit-card debt.

One problem: You've now stretched your credit-card debt over the life of the new mortgage, maybe as long as 30 years. That adds up to a fortune in interest due on all the stuff you charged in the past. To hold down that cost, pay more than the minimum each month, right from the start of the loan.

If a new mortgage would carry a higher interest rate, don't refinance. Turn to a home equity line of credit instead. A credit line gives you borrowing power. You can take a loan against the line whenever you want (up to its maximum) and repay on your own schedule. The interest rate varies, rising and falling along with interest rates in general. The maximum rate is very high (typically more than 20 percent) and there's no cap on how much your payment can rise in any month. So this is a riskier loan whose payments could, potentially, soar.

Don't stretch out home-equity loans, either. Set up a payment schedule that retires them in the shortest possible length of time—preferably two years or less. If you financed your car this way, make automatic repayments at a rate that will clean up the loan before you buy another car.

One tip in shopping for home-equity lines: Don't look just at the introductory interest rate, look at the *margin*. That's the difference between the *prime rate* (the bank's standard rate) and the rate on your loan. With the prime at 6.5 percent, the loan might be priced at prime for an introductory period, then prime plus a margin of 2 percent—adding up to 8.5 percent. That's a better deal than a loan at 6 percent but with a 3 percent margin—for 9 percent in all. Always check the margin even before the rate.

Whatever you pay, home-equity loans are far, far cheaper than credit cards and the interest is tax deductible on loans up to $100,000. As an example, take a $15,000 loan. On a credit card charging 16 percent, you'd owe $2,400 in interest this year. But on a home-equity loan at 6.5 percent, you'd owe just $975. That's a *huge* savings of $1,425—and even more, when you take the tax deduction into consideration. With such a low rate, you could pay off the debt three times faster than if you kept it on your credit card.

Home-equity loans carry fewer closing costs than mortgages do. Some loans have no fees; any costs are included in the rate. Set up only as large a line as you need—too much borrowing power makes you look less creditworthy. After 10 or 15 years, the bank will convert any balance into a limited-term loan with fixed monthly payments. If you sell the house, you have to repay immediately, using some of the proceeds of the sale.

There's a third choice, when borrowing against your home: a fixed-rate home-equity loan, borrowed in a lump sum and payable over a certain term, such as 10, 15, or 20 years. These loans carry higher interest rates but they also offer certainty. Your rate and monthly payment will never change—something budgeters like.

But should you consolidate at all? *No*, if you haven't brought your spending under control. Remember—this is a debt *reduction* plan. If you run up your credit cards again, you'll have saddled yourself with two debts in place of one. And *no*, if you'll be borrowing most or all of your home equity. You might not be able to move if you don't net enough on your home to repay the bank, after selling expenses. And *no*, if you're in financial trouble. When you blow off credit-card bills, you damage your credit; when you blow off your mortgage, you lose your house. Debt consolidation works for careful consumers who had big expenses in the past but have straightened out their financial lives.

THIRD DEBT-BEATER:
AUTOMATE YOUR DEBT-REDUCTION PLAN

Set up fixed, automated, monthly repayments on each of your consumer debts. For debts with low interest rates, base your payments on the current minimum due. For high-rate debts, go with slightly higher payments than you think you can afford (it's worth the stretch). At first your monthly balances won't seem to shrink by very much. But pretty soon, you'll enter a lovely, self-reinforcing cycle, where your debt drops at an ever-steeper pace. That's because, as the debt declines, so does the amount of interest you owe. Every month, more of each payment goes toward reducing principal, which in turn cuts your interest costs even more. As soon as one of your cards is clean, switch that payment to another card.

To see roughly how long it will take to reach Debt Freedom Day, at various monthly payment rates, use one of the calculators on the Web. Three good ones: Bankrate.com, Dinkytown.net, and Choosetosave.org.

A *very* small increase in payments makes an amazing difference to how fast your debt melts away. For example, say you owe $12,000 at 16 percent interest and have been paying $300 a month. That puts your Debt Freedom Day four years and 10 months away.

If you add $100 to every payment, you'll be out of debt in three years and three months. You're a sensible person—you can't afford *not* to spend that extra $100 (it's just $3.30 a day).

Don't be afraid to automate all your debt repayments! You may worry about losing control, but mostly these are bills you're paying anyway—installment loans, car loans, and whatever you're putting toward your credit-card debts. So you might as well automate. Besides, programs on autopilot are far more likely to succeed than those that depend on separate decisions every month. Set up the payments for the date your paycheck clears. If you're paid twice a month, take your mortgage or rent and some of your debt repayments from one paycheck and your savings and remaining debt repayments from the other. If you bank online, it's especially easy to raise or lower the payments until you find a fit.

LAST AND ULTIMATE DEBT-BEATER: LIVE ON THE INCOME THAT REMAINS

Debt has no end, if you keep spending more than the cash you have available. The simplest way to regain control is to pay your daily expenses with cash, check, or debit card (that's your ATM card). You can pay by debit card in any store that takes credit cards. It's like writing a check. The cost of your purchase comes directly out of your bank account.

Once you try cash-y living, you'll discover it's not as hard as you thought. You'll instinctively spend less than you did when you shopped on credit (greenbacks—even plastic greenbacks—feel more real). Besides, you typically spend what you see in your checking account. If you start diverting more of your paycheck toward debt repayment, you'll shrink your household expenses automatically.

I'm not saying that you should cut up your credit cards or put them on ice in your freezer. Lots of us, me included, use credit cards to build rewards—free airline miles, hotel stays, or points toward catalog purchases. No problem, as long as you charge only as much as you can pay in full at the end of the month. If you find that you're charging more, stick with cash, checks, and debit cards until you're out of debt.

A quick word about credit cards with rewards: They give you a lot of value, as long as you pay no annual fee, carry no debt on the card, and actually collect your points or airline miles. Say, for example, that you save for a vacation, put the cost on your card, and pay the bill in full when you return. That's a triple win: You earn interest on the savings, earn points for your credit-card spending, and avoid paying interest, which might have driven up the cost of your vacation by 16 percent or more.

Rewards cards aren't bargains, however, when you keep rolling over your debt every month. You're paying for all those "free miles" in the form of higher interest rates. Many rewards cards also charge annual fees. If your card costs $25 and a frequent-flyer mile is worth one penny, you have to charge $2,500 worth of goods to earn back your fee—and much more than that to be compensated for the interest you're paying on your continuing debt. Card users who always carry debt do better with no-fee, plain-vanilla cards at a lower interest rate.

You'll find the best buys in credit cards today at Cardweb.com. To use cards efficiently, carry just two: (1) A no-fee card, for purchases that you know you can pay in full each month. This can be your rewards card, if you want one. The interest rate shouldn't matter (but look for a low one, just in case a bill or two slops over to another month). Be sure the card has a *grace period*—at least three weeks when no interest will be charged. Otherwise, you'll be paying interest from the day of purchase. (2) A card with a rock-bottom interest rate for big-ticket items that you know you can't pay for all at once. There's usually an annual fee, but most of them are low. I don't see much value in paying higher fees for gold or platinum cards. They come with extra perks but also cost you more—and perks aren't worth anything if you don't use them a lot.

KEEP YOURSELF CREDIT-SHARP

Have you checked your credit history? That's the vast, multiyear record of how fast you pay your bills, how many open accounts you have, how big your credit lines are, and whether you've ever been in real trouble—bill collectors, bankruptcies, judgments, liens. Three credit bureaus—Equifax, Experian, and TransUnion—collect this information from courthouses and various creditors (banks, stores, phone and cable companies, student-loan sources, some medical groups and hospitals). You'll usually have a file at each.

You also have a *credit score*. That's a roundup of your personal debt-repayment history, distilled into a single number by a company called Fair Isaac. It's known as your FICO (Fair Isaac) score. How well you score dictates how much money you can borrow, how high or low your interest rate will be, and whether you'll even be considered for a loan. Super scores run from around 720 to 850; if you're in this group, you'll get mortgages and credit cards at the lowest cost. People who score less than 580 can find loans only at high interest rates, if they qualify at all. In between, you get better rates if you're at the higher end of the range. FICO scores are used not only for approving credit cards and mortgages but also for setting insurance premiums. They may even affect whether you can rent an apartment or get a particular job.

What gets you a good score? The things you'd expect—paying on time and paying off your balances every month. Your score drops when you apply for an additional card or credit line, borrow more against your credit lines, and max out on credit limits. In some scoring systems, you lose points for dealing with finance companies rather than banks and credit unions, and have a lot of department-store charge accounts.

What gets you a bad score? Not paying bills, paying them late, and applying for a lot of new credit all at once. (An exception is made if you're comparison-shopping for a mortgage or auto loan. All such inquiries are counted as one application if you bunch them into a single 14-day period.) If a creditor turns you over to a bill collector, your score takes a hit even though you eventually pay. Black marks stay on your record for seven long years, although creditors pay more attention to how you've behaved in the past year or two.

Credit bureaus create their own scores but creditors generally use FICO. Fair Isaac sells the scores, drawn from the records of each of the bureaus, for $44.85 at this writing (Myfico.com; 800-342-6726).

Credit scores are so important that you dare not chance mistakes in your credit history. Maybe you canceled a credit card but it's still being reported as an open line. That might block you from getting another card at a bargain interest rate. Maybe you disputed—then finally paid—a charge for canceling cell phone service, but it still shows as unpaid on your file. That small item alone might prevent you from qualifying for the lowest mortgage rate.

So please, check your personal record. You're entitled to one free report from each credit bureau every year—available through Annualcreditreport.com (877-322-8228; P.O. Box 105281, Atlanta, GA 30348). You can ask for all three reports at once but it's smarter to stagger them so that you get a report from one of the bureaus every four months. That keeps you up to date on any changes that occur.

If you spot a mistake, report it to the credit bureau on the correction form that comes with your file (report to each bureau separately). The bureau will check with the creditor, which will either confirm or correct the report. Unfortunately, creditors can be pretty sloppy about fixing things. They may reconfirm an error or even reenter it after you thought you'd cleared the problem up. Sometimes consumers have to sue to get a creditor's attention. Courthouses are worse. They may not bother to remove lawsuits or liens that were dropped.

If someone sets up an account in your name, you do have some rights. You can block a retailer or other company from reporting that false account to credit bureaus. You can stop credit bureaus from including fraudulent data in your report. You can also get copies of any documents that the crook signed to open the account. For tips on exercising these rights, here are three good sources: Pirg.org/consumer/credit; Privacyrights.org; and the site of the Federal Trade Commission, Consumer.gov/idtheft. The FTC site includes an excellent free booklet, *Take Charge: Fighting Back Against Identity Theft* (or telephone for a copy at 877-382-4357).

If you suspect you might become a victim of identity theft (perhaps because your credit cards were stolen), you can put a 90-day fraud alert on your credit report and renew it once. A call to just one of the bureaus will flag all three (Equifax, 800-525-6285; Experian, 888-397-3742; TransUnion, 800-680-7289). During that period, creditors aren't supposed to give you new accounts without taking extra steps to verify your identity. If fraud actually occurs, you can extend the alert for seven years. One-year fraud alerts are available to military personnel serving away from home.

Some states now force the credit bureaus to offer you a "security freeze" (for the list, see pirg.org/consumer/credit). A freeze tells the bureaus not to open *any* new credit accounts in your name. To open one yourself, you have to remove the freeze. Removal might take three to five days and you could be charged a fee—so you're saying farewell to "instant credit." Nevertheless, a security freeze gives you peace of mind.

Frequent checks of your credit report give you a better chance of limiting the misuse of your name, although probably not stopping it. Thieves seem to find it simple to break into the data banks, retailers, card-processing companies, colleges, and government bureaus that keep your personal records—stealing credit-card numbers, Social Security numbers, and other identifying data (your mother's maiden name is probably on the Internet, along with the name of your first dog). No one gets fined for maintaining such crummy computer security, so there's little incentive to invest in a major upgrade. You're stuck with the cost and pain of cleaning up the mess yourself. Worse, the mess may never go away. Once your records enter cyberspace, crooks can grab them at any time. They can run up bills in your name, bring down court judgments against you, and even get you arrested. Your horrible record may prevent you from getting future credit. You'll go through hell trying to prove that the bad guy wasn't you.

Any time you're rejected for credit based on a black mark in your credit history, you're supposed to get a letter saying what the problem was. Ditto if you were rejected for employment or insurance, or lose some other advantage such as access to low insurance premiums, low interest rates, or high credit limits. That letter entitles you to free copies of your credit reports. Here's where to call: Equifax at 800-685-1111 (Equifax.com); Experian at 888-397-3742 (Experian.com), or TransUnion at 800-916-8800 (Transunion.com).

If you have an argument with a creditor and refuse to pay a bill, your delinquency goes on your credit report. You can add a short statement telling your side of the story, but it does you no good. Only the black mark is counted in your credit score, not the explanation (infuriating, but true). So you have no leverage; the creditor can take you down. If you're speaking to a lender personally—for example, sitting across the desk from a mortgage banker—you can sometimes overcome the problem. But mortgages also depend on credit scores today, so you're generally stuck.

If you have a child going off to college, be sure to explain about credit reports. Too many students scoop up credit cards as if they were cookies. Then they lose control of their spending or forget about the bill. Late payments could wreck their credit for years—which they won't understand until they get out of school and apply for an auto loan. On the other hand, timely payments will jump-start their grown-up lives. Sign up your kids for free copies of their credit reports, so they can see that you speak true.

FIRST STEPS

If automated debt repayment continues to worry you a little, start with the regular payments you can't avoid—mortgage, car loan, installment loans. Once you've gotten used to them, add the regular payments you make on your credit cards and home-equity lines. Then raise the monthly amounts you pay, to start getting rid of your back debt. Starting more slowly on a repayment program puts off your Debt Freedom Day, but hey, I'm for anything that works!

4. YOUR SAFETY NET

I Don't Really Mean to Scare You, But . . .

For all of us, there's the life we're living and a potential, different life. Our normal days—filled with work, family, friends, shopping, movies, sports, books—are the ordinary way of the world. But down in the dark lies another life that we might have to face if something goes awfully wrong. Fire, accident, sickness, premature death—you hate to think about it and so do I. Life can be so easily turned inside out.

That's the scare (this chapter is the book's scariest). But even during crises, good financial backup systems can support your hopes and dreams. Here, you'll find the most practical ways of weaving yourself a safety net. Once you've done it, you can go back to forgetting that bad stuff exists. If something changes in your life, you simply revisit your protection plan, make a small adjustment, and move on. There's tremendous peace of mind in knowing you can go forward in the face of trouble, or your family can. Here's what you need to be okay:

LIFE INSURANCE

You buy life insurance for just one reason: to support the people who depend on your income if you die prematurely. That's it. Everything else is noise.

Based on that test, it's easy to answer the question, "Do I need insurance?" *No*, if you're single with no children or other dependents. And *no*, if you're married and your spouse would be self-supporting if you died (your spouse might earn enough money to live on, or could live on the assets you'll be leaving behind). In both these cases, you're better off putting your money toward retirement savings. But *absolutely yes*, buy life insurance, lots of it, if anyone relies on you to pay the bills—your children, your spouse, or anyone else you help support. If you're married with no children, but plan to have them soon, buy low-cost coverage now while you're healthy. Kids need the safety of life insurance and you want to be sure that you can provide it.

What kind of insurance should you buy? You want *term insurance*—coverage that lasts for a certain period of time (or "term"). It's plain, simple, and so cheap that you can afford to buy as much of it as your family needs.

All other forms of coverage, generally called *cash-value*, combine life insurance with an investment. Every payment you make has to cover both parts of the policy, so this combo costs you far more than buying insurance all by itself. The investment part, backed with stocks or bonds, is pitched as a way to save for college or retirement. But to get your hands on your money, you either have to cancel the policy (bye-bye, protection), borrow against it (running up interest charges), or withdraw cash directly (which might require you to increase your premiums in the future).

Investing through insurance makes no sense, anyway. It isn't nearly as efficient as the other ways you'll learn about here. Even worse, these policies cost so much that, to stay within a budget, you'd have to buy less life insurance than your family really needs. What's the good of that? You're supposed to be building a safety net. So ignore cash-value policies in all their forms (they're called whole life, universal life, and variable universal life). You need lots of coverage and term is the way to go.

How much life insurance do you need? I vote for using the rule of thumb offered by the Consumer Federation of America: Married couples with two small children need eight times their joint annual income to cover future living expenses for 20 years (nine times earnings for 30 years). Add a fund for college on top of that. Subtract any insurance you get automatically at work. The total gives you the amount to buy. Is this exact? No. But the future is unknowable, so this simple rule is close enough. It assumes that your survivor invests the policy's proceeds conservatively and gradually uses up the money over his or her lifetime. At higher income levels, you might want 10 times income.

To show you how easy it is to decide how much life insurance to buy, here are two examples—one for a $60,000 family, one for a family earning $100,000. In the third column, you can calculate what you need yourself.

You are earning:	$60,000	$100,000	*(Your actual)*
Multiplied by:	× 8	× 10	× ?
Subtotal	$480,000	$1,000,000	_____
Add for college:	+$100,000	+$100,000	_____
Subtract company insurance	−$60,000	−$100,000	_____
Total life insurance needed:	$520,000	$1,000,000	_____

Many sites on the Web will estimate your life insurance needs, based on specific information you supply. A lot of them overestimate (to sell more insurance, natch). My choice: the calculators at Choosetosave.org or Tiaa-Cref.org.

If you're a two-income couple, you both should buy life insurance. Decide on the total the family needs, then divide it between you based on the percentage of family income each of you brings in. For example, if the husband earns 60 percent of the income, he should carry 60 percent of the coverage. If he dies, his policy will replace exactly what he contributed before. The remaining 40 percent of the coverage would be carried by the wife, to replace what she contributes. If the wife earns 70 percent of the total, she should carry 70 percent of the coverage, with the husband insured for the remaining 30 percent.

Here's how to do the calculation. The example below is for an $80,000 family where the husband earns $48,000 and the wife earns $32,000. They want $740,000 worth of life insurance. The column labeled "You" is for your own calculation:

My Example		*You*
What's your total family income?	$80,000	$ _____
Husband earns:	$48,000	$ _____
His percentage of the total:	60%*	_____%*
Wife earns:	$32,000	$ _____
Her percentage of the total:	40%*	_____%*
Total amount of insurance needed:	$740,000	$ _____
The husband's policy:	$444,000 †	$ _____ †
The wife's policy:	$296,000 †	$ _____ †

---

* To get the percentage, divide each spouse's earnings by total family earnings ($100,000).
† Multiply the total amount of insurance needed by the percentage of the family income that each spouse earns. Buyers should round up the numbers to whole amounts, making it $450,000 for the husband and $300,000 for the wife.

If you're a one-income couple, the breadwinner should carry all the life insurance. The family depends on that single check. Don't buy less coverage than you need, expecting your spouse to make up the difference by getting a job. What if he or she can't? And what about the kids? No one should plan on leaving a spouse with a harder life, especially when term insurance is so cheap.

Insurance companies offer volume discounts—lower prices per $1,000 on policies exceeding a certain size. Typical price points (or "break points"): $250,000, $500,000, $750,000, and $1 million. If you need something close to these amounts, consider raising your coverage to get the better price.

Should you buy life insurance on a spouse who takes care of the kids full-time? The answer isn't cut-and-dried. If one of you is home with young kids and dies, the survivor may have to pay for child care. A policy on the at-home spouse would help cover the cost. On the other hand, maybe you could pay for child care out of your regular paycheck; your money goes further when there's one less person in the house. (I'm not being coldhearted here, just practical.) If so, it's better to put extra money into a retirement account rather than buy spouse insurance.

If you opt for the coverage, follow these two rules: (1) Buy all the insurance the breadwinner needs before adding a policy on the spouse. Family protection always comes first. (2) The spouse policy should last only as long as the children will need care—maybe five or ten years—and should cover only that expense. If you figure $10,000 a year for day care, over five years, the spouse policy would come to $50,000.

Should you buy your term insurance through your employer? Large companies offer you some free insurance—often a policy that equals one year's salary. You can buy more through payroll deduction, but should you? *Yes*, if you're in poor health—it's probably the best deal you can get. Otherwise, I give this idea a qualified *maybe*. Buy the coverage only if it meets all of the following conditions:

- *Its price is low.* Check the cost of individual term policies at the online quote services, Term4sale.com and Insure.com. You may find cheaper policies than the one your company offers, especially if you're young.

- *It's portable.* You want to be able to take the term policy with you if you leave your job. That's really important. If your health turns bad, a portable policy may be the only insurance you can get at a decent price. Some companies require you to switch to expensive cash-value insurance if you want to take the policy with you. No, no, no—that's not coverage you want. You probably won't be able to buy enough of it. Conversion to cash-value coverage should be an option but not a must.

- *It's convertible to cash-value insurance.* Term insurance you buy through your company should be convertible to cash-value coverage *if* you want it, at some future date. After dissing cash values, I probably sound crazy for insisting that you should have the option. But there are a handful of circumstances where it really works (pages 62–63). You want this option open, even if you never use it.

Your company benefits department can tell you how the employee policy works. If it doesn't meet these three tests, buy your own, personal policy from an insurance company.

Should you buy term insurance through a trade group or professional association? All the questions that apply to employee insurance apply here, too. You want low-cost, portable term coverage, convertible to cash-value if you want to switch. If the policy can't deliver, buy your insurance independently.

Did you know you had government life insurance? If you die and you're covered by Social Security, your family will receive monthly benefits. Checks go to: your children under 18, or under 19 if they're still in high school; your disabled children over 18 if they became disabled before age 22; a spouse who's caring for children under 16 or disabled; and a spouse who's at least 60 (50, if he or she is disabled). Spouses with earnings, however, will have their benefits reduced. For details, see ssa.gov/pubs.

BUYING INDIVIDUAL TERM INSURANCE

The industry has made buying term insurance super-easy today, thanks to the Web. You can check prices there, buy a policy online, or find an agent who will sell you the policy that you've priced in advance. Here's a quick checklist to help you make the right insurance decision.

- *The policy term.* Most term insurance today is sold for fixed periods of time: typically, 5 years, 10 years, 15 years, 20 years, or 30 years. It's called *level-term* insurance. The longer the term, the higher the annual premium (the "premium" is the price you pay). During the years that you hold the policy, your price won't change.

  Buy coverage for the longest period you can imagine needing it—usually until retirement. A 35-year-old man in excellent but not perfect health might pay $380 a year for a $500,000 policy lasting 20 years, and $564 for a policy lasting 30 years. That extra ten years costs him only $15 a month—for his family, worth every penny. A 35-year-old woman might pay $335 a year for a 20-year policy and $484 for a 30-year guarantee—just $12 more a month. Ideally, when the term is up, you won't need life insurance any more. Your kids will be gone and you'll have enough savings for you and your spouse to live on.
- *Whether the policy is convertible.* Be sure that the term policy can be converted into cash-value coverage, in case you need it. Sometimes you do—especially if you have to renew your policy when your health is bad (see below). There are other, more re-

mote possibilities. One such: You have a disabled child. To provide for that child, you'll need insurance that lasts for as long as you live, even to age 100, at a fixed cost. That's something only a cash-value policy can provide. Another such: You're plenty rich and want to leave your children even more than they'd get now. By converting your policy from term to cash-value, you can leave them the proceeds tax-free. Check on the term policy's conversion terms. Some let you convert only within the policy's first five years; others give you 10 years, or for the length of the level-pay period, or to age 65. The longer the better.

• *Renewing the policy.* When you buy term insurance, you're hoping that you won't need it by the time the policy expires. Your kids will be grown and you'll have enough saved for your spouse to live on if you die. Or you'll be single and won't have anyone to protect.

But there's a chance that you'll need life insurance for longer than you thought. Maybe you married late and have young children. Maybe you used or lost your savings through bad luck or bad investments and have to keep working to help support a spouse. If you want to extend your level-term coverage you have three choices, two of them affordable and one for desperation only:

1. *If you're in good health (or good enough):* Shop for new level-term insurance. You'll have to pass a medical exam. A 55-year-old man can buy $500,000 worth of 10-year term for $985 a year if he's in excellent shape and $1,450 if he's average. You might find acceptable coverage even if your health is subpar.

2. *If you're in poor health:* Convert your term policy to cash-value insurance. There's no medical exam. Cash-value coverage is much more expensive than term but you can cap the cost by buying less of it. At 55, a $200,000 policy, at cur-

rent interest rates, might cost a low of $3,500 a year for the type of coverage known as no-lapse universal life (the premium is guaranteed not to rise). Good timing is important! You must convert within the time period that the policy allows. Check this with your insurance agent or read the policy yourself. If you wait too long, you lose your chance.

3. *If you're in poor health and missed your chance to convert to cash-value coverage:* You can renew your expiring level-term coverage without a health exam but only at incredibly high premiums. Worse, the cost jumps every year. Even for a $200,000 policy, our 55-year-old man would pay $3,200 the first year, $8,500 by age 65, and $23,500 by 75. That's worth doing only at death's door. If you know you'll need coverage well into the future and see that you won't be able to pass a health exam, convert your term policy to cash-value coverage while you still can.

- *Your annual premium.* All term insurance does *not* cost the same, as many people think. The price differences among companies are huge. You can save hundreds, even thousands, of dollars by spending five minutes comparison-shopping on the Web. As an example, take a 35-year-old man, a nonsmoker in excellent health, buying a 30-year term policy worth $500,000. A low-priced insurer might charge him $564 a year. A high-priced insurer might charge $1,189—and for exactly the same product! If he's in average health, he could pay as little as $855 or as much as $1,700, depending on the insurance company (and insurance agent) he chooses. The older you get, the wider the price difference. At 50, a man in excellent health might pay as little as $2,220 or as much as $4,515. The lower-priced company saves him up to $2,294 a year. Women live longer, on average, so their insurance doesn't cost as much. Still, they face the same price spread. At 35, a woman in excellent health might buy this policy for as little as $484 or as much as $915. Why would anyone pay the higher price? Because he or she didn't shop. Or because the agent claimed that the expensive company was worth it. That's pure baloney. You can get excellent service at top-rated companies that charge consumers less.

Prices vary from state to state and from day to day, so your price won't be exactly what I've quoted here. But you get the idea. For your own quote, go to Term4sale.com—a site that sifts through the prices offered by 150 insurers and gives you a range of costs in seconds. You can also ask for the names of three nearby insurance agents who will sell you the policy you've chosen (be sure you insist on term; don't let them deflect you to cash-value coverage). Another quote site, Insure.com, will connect you with a life insurance agent online. You might find a lower rate if you live in one of the eleven states where the Savings Bank Life Insurance Company of Massachusetts sells policies. For a quote, go to Sbli.com or call 888-GET-SBLI. Two other direct sellers to check: USAA Life (800-531-8000) and Ameritas Direct at Ameritasdirect.com (800-555-4655).

You'll find many other insurance-sales websites. Most are referral sites for insurance agents who rarely offer the lowest-cost coverage. They often ask for your phone number (a no-no, when you're using the Web just for price comparisons). You'll run into a lot of incomplete or misleading information, including the idea that policies are cheaper online (they cost the same, whether sold by Web or across your kitchen table). If you stick with the sites I've suggested, you'll do fine.

All the premiums I've quoted are guaranteed for the life of the policy. You can also buy nonguaranteed level-term insurance with premiums fixed only for the first few years. After that, they might stay the same or rise, depending on what the insurance company decides. Nonguaranteed policies are cheaper at the start but personally I wouldn't touch them. Your rate *might* rise, especially if the company is sold. If that happened, people in good health would promptly switch to cheaper insurers, meaning even higher rates for those who are left behind. Believe me, you don't want to get stuck.

If you've never shopped for life insurance or haven't shopped for years, fire up your computer and look. You may find a cheaper policy than the one you have now, making it worth your while to switch. If you can afford it, pay the premiums annually instead of monthly. Annual payments save your money.

- *Your premium and your age.* The older you are, the more you pay when you buy life insurance. But at later ages, you usually need less coverage and for shorter terms, so you can probably still afford to buy whatever you need. At 60, a man in excellent health might pay just $900 a year for a $200,000, 10-year policy. If he still needs $500,000 (late marriage, young children), he might get a 20-year policy for $3,500 a year. In short, there's enough level term around to cover people of all ages who might reasonably need it—always provided that you stay in decent health.

- *Your premium and your health.* The size of your premium depends on the state of your health. The best rates go to "preferred" and "excellent" risks. But even if you're rated "average," term insurance is cheap. A $500,000, 30-year policy might cost a 40-year-man in average health just $1,300 a year (I'm always quoting the lowest-cost insurance companies). What kills you is smoking—speaking only financially, of course. A smoker policy would cost our guy $3,100 a year. Your price also jumps if you're overweight, have high blood pressure or high cholesterol, or a chronic condition such as diabetes.

  You can get small amounts of insurance—maybe $25,000 to $150,000—without a medical exam. But that doesn't mean that the insurer doesn't care about your health. You have to answer questions about your medical history, medications you take, and any conditions that you're currently dealing with. Don't lie!

Liars don't get paid, if they make a claim within the first two years and the insurer investigates (after two years, your policy is generally impregnable). Your application will also be checked against any records you have at the Medical Information Bureau—a database that consumers need to know about. Insurers send MIB any test results or treatment records that, in their opinion, suggest you might be a health risk. This includes records from health exams you've taken for life, health, long-term care, or disability insurance within the past seven years, as well as information that insurers get from your doctor (you approve the release of your records when you apply for coverage). To check your file for accuracy, call MIB at 866-692-6901 or apply through its website, Mib.com. It's free.

For larger amounts of insurance, you'll need a health exam. The insurer will send a paramedic to your home or office for a blood test, urine test, and blood-pressure reading. If you've had health problems, you may need to take a more extensive physical and provide a statement from your doctor. People in tricky health need a life insurance agent who specializes in finding coverage for "impaired risks."

- *Your insurance company.* Choose one with high ratings for safety and soundness. For conservative buyers, that's a rating of A+ or up (very conservative buyers want A++ or A+++). You'll find the company's rating on the price-quote websites.

A different type of term insurance—great for younger people. These policies, called *annually renewable term (ART)*, have one key virtue—they never expire. They're automatically renewable to age 80 and higher, at regular rates and with no further medical exams. ART premiums go up every year. For the first few years, you pay less than you'd have paid for level-term. Eventually, you start paying more. But you never get an extra boost in price because your health goes bad.

I think annually renewable term is terrific for younger people. Buy it when you're, say, under 35. At 35, you can switch to one of the low-cost, 30-year level-term policies, if your health is still good. If it's not, you can keep the ART policy for as long as you need it. This strategy keeps you safely insured to 65. By contrast, if you buy a 30-year policy when you're in your twenties or early thirties, it will expire before you reach retirement age. That could cause problems, if your health turns poor.

Other forms of life insurance. Don't bother with mortgage insurance (to pay off your mortgage immediately if you die); accident insurance (for extra coverage on the off chance you die in an accident); or credit insurance (to pay off your credit-card debts). Dollar for dollar, they're hugely expensive. Your term-life policy will cover all your obligations, including the monthly mortgage payments. Put your money toward your retirement investments, instead.

AN INSTANT GUIDE TO TERM INSURANCE

1. Multiply your income by 8 (or 10) and subtract any life insurance you get at work. The remainder is the size policy you need.

2. If you're 35 and up, check Term4sale.com and Insure.com for quotes on level, convertible term.

3. If you're under 35, check the cost of annually renewable term at Tiaa-Cref.org, Sbli.com, or USAA (800-531-8000). Buy through any of these organizations or ask an insurance agent to beat the quote (unlikely, but you can ask). At 35, switch to 30-year level-term, if your health is good enough to qualify at preferred rates. Some people might want to hold ART until age 45 and then buy 20-year or 30-year level-term. It all depends on your personal circumstances and price.

HEALTH INSURANCE

If you can get health insurance at work, you're a lucky duck. The amount you pay toward the cost will keep rising but at least you're covered, which is more than 46 million other people can say.

With no employee plan, you face a harsher world. Individual health insurance is seriously expensive. As the years go by, your premiums will rise. Past or present illnesses may be excluded from coverage. If you've had an ailment that the insurer doesn't like, you may not get coverage at all. Yet without health insurance, an accident or illness that fells you, your spouse, or your child could wipe you out.

There's an option, if you're insurable but can't afford comprehensive coverage. Go for a "catastrophic" policy. It requires you to pay all the smaller bills but protects against the Big One.

As you search for health insurance, you'll find five broad types.

1. *HMOs (health maintenance organizations).* Good for young families that need routine care. Premiums are low (at least "low" as health policies go); your cash payment for every doctor visit (the co-pay) may run no higher than $10 or $15, and you generally don't have to pay a portion of every bill. You'll pick a primary-care doctor, who will refer you—as needed—to specialists within the group. The insurance pays only for doctors and hospitals in the plan, except for emergency care. For a higher price, the HMO might offer a point of service (POS) option. That gives you limited coverage for doctors outside the plan. If you see outside doctors, however, you'll have to pay a higher percentage of the bill.

2. *PPOs (preferred provider organizations).* The best deal for people who want to see specialists and get medical tests with-

out referrals. You have more of a hand in directing your care, at the price of higher premiums and co-pays. PPOs offer larger networks of doctors than you'll get at an HMO. If you see a doctor outside the network, you'll pay a higher percentage of the cost. As you've probably noticed, you need an above-average income to afford a PPO.

3. *Indemnity plans.* For people who don't care what their health care costs. You can see any doctor for any procedure. But you'll typically pay 20 percent of whatever cost the insurance company deems "correct." If the doctor charges more than that, you pay the additional amount.

4. *Catastrophic coverage.* For people who can't afford a comprehensive plan but want to protect themselves from a wipeout. You pay all your medical bills up to a certain ceiling—say, $2,000, $5,000, or $10,000, whichever you pick. The insurer picks up most of the rest. The higher the deductible, the lower your monthly premiums. Parents sometimes buy high-deductible coverage for young-adult children who can't afford health insurance on their own.

5. *Special coverage for children.* The State Children's Health Insurance Program, for people with modest incomes. Premiums are low (sometimes zero). Check it out, if you have no employer plan or can't afford the family coverage that your employer offers. You'll find information at www.cms.hhs.gov/schip and insurekidsnow.gov, or toll-free at 1-877-KIDS-NOW (1-877-543-7669).

Tips for Employees with Company Plans

Slash your out-of-pocket costs with a health-care flexible spending account. Most of the larger companies offer one. Flexible spending accounts cut your personal medical costs by 15 to 35 percent (and sometimes more!) because you're paying with dollars you receive tax-free. Nevertheless—to my constant surprise—most employees don't sign up. They shrug and throw this free money away. If you have access to a flexible spending account and aren't using it, make this the week you change your ways. All you have to do is call your company's employee benefits department. You may not be able to start right away. The plans generally open for enrollment at year-end or whenever you've had a major life change such as marriage or childbirth. But you can take the first step—finding out about the plan—at any time. Here's how they work:

Your company deducts a fixed sum from each paycheck and deposits it into a personal account (you name the sum, anywhere from a small amount up to a typical maximum of $3,000 to $5,000 a year). You use that money for medical and dental bills that your insurance doesn't cover—the co-pays and deductibles, as well as such things as teeth cleaning, laser eye surgery, cosmetic surgery, over-the-counter medications, and premiums for long-term care insurance (page 83). Your employee benefits office will tell you what's eligible.

There's one minor hitch: In every year, you have to spend all the money deposited in your health-care account by a certain date—either December 31 or March 15 of the following year. Any cash left over reverts to the company. But you'll be fine as long as you plan. You might start by contributing half the money you spent out-of-pocket last year, to get a feel for how the program works. Once you're pretty sure that you won't get stuck with money left over, you can raise your contribution. Raise it, too, in a year you intend to have your teeth capped or your eyes fixed. You can always cut back the following year. As the annual deadline approaches, check your account and start spending any remaining money on evergreens such as prescription sunglasses and over-the-counter medications. You have to document your spending when you tap the account, so keep the receipts.

Use COBRA to maintain your health insurance—for yourself

and your family—when you leave a group plan. COBRA* is bridge insurance. It lets you continue your current group health plan for a limited period of time while you hunt for other coverage. You pay the premiums out-of-pocket at the group rate plus 2 percent— *never* letting the words "too expensive" cross your lips. It's potentially far more expensive not to be insured. You're entitled to COBRA if you work for a company that employs 20 people or more. Government workers get COBRA, too. Unfortunately, this safety net doesn't extend to people who buy health coverage through a trade association. If they leave the association, they lose their group rates. The same is usually true if you leave a company that employs fewer than 20 people, although some will extend your group policy for a few more months (in a few states, they have to).

Who might use COBRA to keep his or her group-health insurance going? Fired employees looking for work; employees who quit a job to start their own business; employees who lose coverage because they dropped from full-time to part-time work; early retirees; young adults leaving a parent's plan; widows and widowers formerly covered by their late spouse's plan; spouses losing coverage after a divorce or legal separation; spouses losing coverage because their mate switched from the company plan to Medicare; and domestic partners with the equivalent of spouse benefits. That's a lot of people who stand to gain.

COBRA coverage lasts for up to 18 months, if you quit your job, lose it, or go part-time (some plans give you even more than 18 months). You get up to 29 months if you're totally disabled, although at a higher cost and only with a letter from Social Security. Divorced spouses, widows and widowers, and their dependents get up to 36 months.

Important facts about deadlines! You have a limited number of

---

* "COBRA" comes from the law that authorized this benefit, the Consolidated Omnibus Budget Reconciliation Act.

days to notify the insurer that you want COBRA. If you wait too long, you're out of luck. Here are the deadlines: 60 days, if you're losing coverage because of a divorce or legal separation; 30 days, if it's due to a death or because the policyholder switched to Medicare (that's an especially tight time limit for someone suffering the loss of a spouse). If you leave your job or one of your children gets too old to stay on your policy, your employer is supposed to tell the insurance company. The insurer then sends you a letter asking if you want to buy the continuing coverage. You have 60 days to reply. Don't wait. If you have no other insurance lined up, say *yes*.

Safeguard your access to future health insurance, if you have a health problem (or someone in your family does) and you leave your job. This is critical! If you have, say, diabetes or serious allergies, and you leave your group health plan, another insurer might not want to pick you up. Or it might take you but refuse to cover that particular illness, or impose a "waiting period" before coverage starts. The same thing could happen if your spouse or one of your kids is sick. Happily, there are rules that protect you from health discrimination but you have to know about them and follow through. These rules also help spouses and children who lose coverage after a divorce or because the family breadwinner died.

The law that preserves your access to health insurance is known as HIPPA (Health Insurance Portability and Accountability Act). It applies to people leaving group-health plans and looking for new group or individual insurance. Under HIPPA, the new company can't turn you down or charge you more because your health is poor. It's also not allowed to impose a waiting period before covering your "preexisting conditions"—defined as health problems that were diagnosed or treated in the six months before you applied for the policy.

HIPPA operates through a piece of paper called a "Certification of Creditable Coverage." You get it from your company when you leave the job. The certificate states how long you've been insured and which family members were on your policy. Your new insurer will check it, to see how much protection you're entitled to. Here are the rules:

If you move to another employer's group health plan right away: You must be accepted for full coverage, regardless of health, as long as you were previously insured for at least 12 months. (That jumps to 18 months if you fail to join the new health plan as soon as you're hired, so sign up instantly.) If you were covered for less than 12 months, your new group plan can impose a short waiting period before accepting a preexisting condition (except for pregnancy, which has to be covered).

If it takes a while to land a new job. You lose your HIPPA protection if you've been without group health coverage for more than 63 days. When you eventually find work, your new company will be allowed to wait up to 12 months before including your preexisting conditions in its health insurance plan. In most cases, the company will cover you anyway, but you're taking a risk. Best advice: Buy COBRA insurance to cover the period you're looking for work. That's a group plan and it preserves your eligibility for HIPPA.

If you're leaving a group plan, or your COBRA coverage is ending, and you have to buy your own individual or family health insurance: You must be accepted, regardless of health, as long as you were previously insured for at least 18 months *and* you buy new coverage right away. I'm shouting here—get that policy fast! If you wait for more than 63 days before buying new insurance, you'll lose your HIPPA protection. That could be a disaster if you or anyone in your family has health problems—even small ones. Without HIPPA to help, insurers in most states can refuse to sell you a policy or refuse to cover health conditions you've had in the past, even the distant past. Please, please don't get stuck. (Note: Insurers are required to sell you a policy in New Jersey, New York, and Vermont. That's a godsend for people in poor health, although it raises the premiums for people in good health.)

If you're dropping an individual health insurance policy and buying another one: You have no HIPPA protection. A new insurer can refuse to cover any preexisting health conditions. The market for individual coverage is a scandal. The pits.

Expect your employer to start selling you on the idea of "consumer-driven care." In truth, there's nothing "consumer" about it. These new plans are designed to slash the amount of money that companies spend on health insurance. That means shifting more of the medical bill to you.

Each company shapes its plan in a different way. But in general, they work like this: You pay the first $500 or $1,000 in medical costs each year. And each year, the company deposits $1,000 to $2,000 into a personal medical savings account for your additional expenses. If your bills are low, the money in the account accumulates tax-deferred. If your bills exceed what's in the account, you pay the next $1,500 to $2,000 yourself. Insurance covers 80 percent or 90 percent of any further costs. You might also be able to contribute to a tax-free Health Savings Account and use that money to cover your share of the bills.

At most companies today, the consumer-driven plan is one of several options. You might choose it because the annual premiums are low and you're healthy enough to think you'll be able to save at least some of the money you're allotted every year. Nevertheless, you're gambling. If you get seriously sick, or someone in your family does, you'll burn through that company allotment in a hurry. Typically, your backup insurance won't pay as much as your former, comprehensive plan did. If your illness continues, however, you might have the option of switching to better coverage in the following year.

You would *not* choose this plan if you have a chronic illness. You'd be paying the full out-of-pocket amount year after year, which adds up to more than the cost of the higher premium for better coverage. Avoid "consumer" plans, too, if you're a heart-attack risk or if a costly medical condition runs in your family.

Over time, the new plans will undermine traditional, comprehensive coverage. They'll attract the healthier employees, leaving only those with illnesses in the older plan. Premiums for the older plan will soar. Already, lower-paid workers are opting out of employee health insurance because the premiums are too high. Workers in the mid-pay ranges may eventually be forced out, too. You may wind up choosing "consumer" care because it's all you can afford.

Expect the arrival of "limited-benefits" policies. They'll provide access to medical care but pay only a low fixed dollar amount toward a specified number of doctor visits, lab tests, or prescription drugs. The best to be said for a limited-benefit policy is that it's better than nothing, if nothing is the alternative.

Tips for Buying Individual Health Insurance

Shrink your health insurance premiums by buying high-deductible "catastrophic" coverage. If you're self-employed or have no employee plan, this may be the only kind of policy you can afford. You're covered for serious illnesses but have to pay the lesser bills yourself. The higher the upfront deductible (usually, anywhere from $2,000 to $10,000), the lower the premium you pay.

Shop the Web for policies. Many state websites list health insurance companies and compare their premium costs. You'll also see ads on billboards or in the Yellow Pages. HMOs generally sell directly to consumers by mail or phone. Other health insurers sell through insurance agents—ask your friends for the name of an agent they'd recommend. You can get sample quotes at Ehealthinsurance.com.

If you're self-employed, another option is the Health Savings

Account (HSA). It combines high-deductible, catastrophic health insurance with a tax-favored savings plan. For the insurance part of the plan, you pick a deductible. That's the amount you're willing to pay out-of-pocket each year. It typically runs between $1,000 and $5,000 for individuals and $2,000 to $10,000 for families. The insurer pays most of the bills over that amount.

You pay the lesser bills—and that's where the savings part of the plan comes in. You make a tax-deductible contribution* every year to a special HSA account. When the medical bills arrive, you pay them out of that account, tax-free. Unspent money stays in your HSA in a year when your medical bills are light.

This raises the question of what you do with the unspent money in your HSA. As a practical matter, you'll probably want to keep it in a bank account or money-market mutual fund so it will be on hand to cover medical bills. Unfortunately, you may lose money on that arrangement. The annual fee for your HSA could exceed the interest earned in your account. Alternatively, you could invest in stocks or bonds (usually, mutual funds). But how will you pay your medical bills in a year when the market drops and your account loses money? None of your choices are terrific.

The attraction of HSAs is that they reduce the premium you pay for health coverage, because you're buying less insurance. Whether they also lower the total you spend on medical care depends on how healthy you and your family are. A serious or chronic illness will use up all your savings and then some. In this respect, they resemble the consumer-driven group health plans that employers offer, but HSAs are for people who are paying all the bills themselves.

Health Savings Accounts work best if (1) you're rarely sick and can build up big reserves; (2) you have enough money to pay your medical bills from your current income and can treat the HSA as if

---

* Contribution ranges for 2006: $1,000 to $2,700 for an individual; $2,000 to $5,450 for a family; and an extra $700 if you're 55 and up. Those ceilings increase every year.

it were a tax-deferred retirement account. If you're interested, talk to an insurance agent.

Turn to an insurance agent if you've had poor health. An insurance company may reject you for reasons that astound you—say, seasonal allergies, an old knee injury, or current treatment for depression (so much for "Prozac Nation"). Or they may accept you but refuse to cover certain conditions, or refuse to cover them for several months or years. They may also charge you more. If you've had an illness that the insurer doesn't like, such as diabetes or heart disease, you might not get coverage at all. You need a good insurance agent, one who specializes in impaired risks, to find the best coverage available.

Buy insurance now, *even if you can afford only high-deductible catastrophic coverage.* Insurers get tighter every year about the kinds of health risks they're willing to accept. The younger you are, the healthier you're apt to be and the easier to insure. And you never know. Next week, something might happen—an accident, an unexpected diagnosis—that makes insurance impossible to get.

Expect your premiums to go up. Insurers are notorious for raising the premiums on individual coverage. They can't target you alone but can increase the price of your entire class of policies. Your best bet: Buy from a large and established health plan, even if it costs more at the start. Its prices will rise with the rate of medical inflation but perhaps not any faster. Smaller insurers whose prices seem low are more apt to jack up premiums at high double-digit rates.

Dig out any overcharges. Checking hospital bills for mistakes is a major pain, but errors and overcharges can run to thousands of dollars. Ask for an itemized statement and give it the sniff test. Question the hospital and your doctor if something looks odd (don't feel foolish asking; people do it all the time, and many hospitals offer free help desks). Raise questions, too, if your insurer rejects a claim. Each health procedure has its own code number. Maybe your health provider entered the wrong one. If your medical bills are large enough, it may be worthwhile to hire someone to check them out and collect what, if anything, you're owed. Two places to find professional help: Claims.org and Billadvocates.com. Typical charge: $30 an hour.

An Important Tip for Everyone

To hold down costs, you probably try to use doctors who belong to your health plan's network. But when you're in the hospital, an out-of-network doc or technician might be brought into your case without your knowing. This could be a consulting surgeon during a complicated operation, a neonatal specialist for a premature birth, an anesthesiologist, or a radiologist, among others. If your case is an emergency, your plan should pick up its usual share of the bill. If not, you'll have to pay the out-of-network charge, even though it's something you didn't authorize. Patients who can plan ahead should tell their docs to stick with professionals who accept their insurance plan.

PRESCRIPTION-DRUG INSURANCE

Most employer plans today offer three-tier coverage for prescription drugs. You might pay just $10 toward the cost of a generic drug, $20 for a brand-name drug that doesn't have a generic version, and $30 or more (as much as $100!) if you opt for a brand name when a generic is available. Alternatively, your cost might be a fixed percentage of the price, which means you pay more for expensive drugs. You can often cut the price or the co-pay by buying medications through your plan's mail-order service.

If you're not covered by insurance, finding discounts is a must. Compare the cost of generic drugs at various pharmacies. Many customers don't realize that markups vary widely from store to store. You might find the lowest generic prices at the pharmacies run by discount outlets such as Costco and Sam's Club. Web sources include Drugstore.com, CVS.com, and Walgreens.com. For the name of generic alternatives to branded drugs and an explanation of any differences, go to Rxaminer.com.

For brand-name drugs, look north. Canadian pharmacies generally offer the lowest prices, even after shipping. You'll find all the famous names—Allegra, Fosamax, Lipitor, Premarin, Prozac, and Viagra, to mention just a few—certified for safety by the Therapeutic Products Directorate, Canada's version of the U.S. Food and Drug Administration. Among the many online pharmacies: Canadadrugs.com, Canarx.com, Doctorsolve.com, Universaldrugstore.com, and Hometownmeds.com.

Delete the online cheap-drug spam that clogs your e-mail. It might promise Ambien with no prescription needed, but the drug you receive isn't Ambien and probably comes from India or Indonesia. It may work because it's an Ambien knockoff, but you don't know whether it's really safe. Some drugs are fine, others total phonies. I don't like the risk.

For Medicare beneficiaries, the government introduced Part D—prescription drug insurance—in January 2006. For details, see Medicare.gov. You can skip the coverage if you're protected by a retiree policy. But consider it if you're uninsured, even if you use few drugs. If you buy Part D later than your eligibility date, you'll be charged an extra 1 percent for each month of delay.

DISABILITY INSURANCE

The one thing most of us never insure is our earning power. And yet it's our most important asset. If you fall off a roof and wind up in a wheelchair, how are you going to pay the bills? That's what disability insurance is for. It pays you a regular benefit—say, $3,000 or $5,000 a month—if you're too sick or injured to earn a paycheck or can't earn as much as you did before. If you have to work for a living and have no disability insurance, you don't have a financial plan. You're a circus act without a net.

If you're covered by an employee-benefit plan, you may be offered the option of buying group long-term disability coverage. Give a lot of thought to saying yes. Group coverage does have a couple of drawbacks. You usually can't take the policy with you if you go to another job. After the first two years, it might pay only if you're totally disabled, not if you're partly disabled and can work part-time. But the price is right. Group coverage costs far less than comparable individual coverage sold on the open market.

If you can afford it, however, go for individual coverage. So it costs a little more; so what? If you're married, good disability coverage could save your spouse and kids from poverty. If you're single, it could keep you from becoming a ward of the state.

Having scared you again, I can now say that there's an easy way out. Call an insurance agent (ask your friends for recommendations). Disability coverage isn't like term insurance that you can shop for alone. These policies are pocked with holes. If you have even a teeny health problem, the insurer might exclude it from coverage, give you less coverage than you want, or raise your rate. It takes a good agent to sort through what's available. Here are the main points to consider:

- *How much coverage do I need?* Enough to provide a decent standard of living if you couldn't work. Single people need more than people with working spouses. Insurers won't sell you a policy that replaces your entire income. Most people can buy up to 60 or 70 percent of their total income, including income from side jobs. High earners might get 40 percent.

- *When am I considered disabled?* This is critical. Low-cost policies pay only if you're totally disabled and can't work at all. But most disabled people can theoretically work at *something* whether they find a job or not, so your claim could be denied. No good. You want a policy that pays if you can't work in your own occupation (or "own occ"). Look for the type of own-occ coverage called "income replacement." This type of policy will pay when you can't do your usual work. If you find a lesser-paid job and choose to take it, some portion of your earnings will be subtracted from your disability check.

- *How long will the policy pay?* Ideally, you want to be covered until retirement age, usually 65. If that costs too much, a policy that pays for five years will cover most disabilities. Still, that leaves your family at risk.

- *What if I can work only part-time?* Your policy should pay residual benefits, giving you, say, half a disability check if you're working half-time. You shouldn't be forced to work full-time, unless you're well enough to manage.

- *How long do I have to wait before the policy starts to pay?* Three months is the most popular waiting period, although you can lower the cost by agreeing to wait for 6 or 12 months. Longer periods make sense if you have enough income or assets to pay your bills in the meantime.

- *Can my premium go up?* Supposedly, your price is fixed for the life of the policy. The insurance company isn't allowed to single you out for a premium increase because you got older or got sick. But if it decides that the policy isn't profitable enough, it can raise premiums for everyone across the board—so "fixed" prices actually do rise.

- *Can the insurance company cancel my coverage?* Look for coverage that's guaranteed renewable—meaning that the company has to renew it every year.

- *Can I cut costs?* Consider "annually renewable" disability insurance. The premiums start low and rise every year, which you can afford if your income rises, too. By middle age, however, this form of coverage gets expensive. At some point, you'd probably want to convert to a fixed-price policy that's guaranteed renewable.

- *Can I get insurance when I'm older?* Sure, if you can pass the physical and can afford the premium. Most insurers even let working people keep their policies after 65, although, if you're disabled, they'll pay benefits only for a single year.

- *What if I'm self-employed and work at home?* It's almost impossible for you to get individual disability coverage. Insurers can't easily tell when you're truly unable to work. Sometimes, however, part of your income may be insurable—for example, income from seminars you give. You might find minimal group coverage through a business or professional association.

- *What if I retire early?* If you have no earnings, cancel your disability insurance. The policy covers loss of pay. No pay, no coverage.

In the worst case, you have some automatic coverage. There's workers' compensation for work-related injuries (varying by state, with low dollar ceilings); veterans' insurance, if your disability arose at least partly from something that happened while you were on active duty; and Social Security, if you're totally disabled. Check the size of your potential Social Security benefit on the annual statement that the government sends you three months before your birthday every year. (Do you even know you get this statement? Millions of people just stare at the envelope and throw it out.) There are benefits for dependents, too.

AUTO AND HOMEOWNER'S INSURANCE

I won't dwell on this. You know you need it. Your state and your mortgage lender say you have to have it. An insurance agent helps you find it. You also can get good quotes on the Web.

Auto Insurance

Shop around! It couldn't be easier, thanks to the Web. You'll find that different insurers quote widely different prices for exactly the same coverage. A good, low-cost company could save you hundreds of dollars a year. Start your search at your state's website—many states publish buyer's guides that list the premiums all the insurers charge. Then check the quotes at Insure.com and compare them with what's on offer online at Progressive, GEICO, State Farm, and Allstate.

You need: (1) A significant amount of liability coverage, in case you injure someone or do major property damage. (2) Zero or minimal medical-payments coverage if you already have health insurance. (3) Collision insurance, for accidents, and comprehensive insurance, for random damage and theft, if your car is pretty new. (But not if the car is old—the insurer won't pay any more to fix or replace it than its fair market value.) The higher the deductible you choose, the less this portion of your policy costs. (4) A significant amount of uninsured and underinsured motorist coverage, in case you're injured or disabled by a hit-and-run or someone with no or insufficient coverage.

Don't settle for the state's minimum policy amount if you have substantial assets. It's *remotely* possible that some day you might fall asleep at the wheel and cause a terrible accident. Without enough insurance, you'd have to sell your investments, mortgage your house, and forfeit part of your future earning power. You'd need a large policy to pay that judgment for you. Remote but potentially devastating risks are what insurance is for.

When you apply for coverage, tell the truth about your past accidents. The insurer will check your story against a database called CLUE (the Comprehensive Loss Underwriting Exchange), which lists all the claims you've made over the past five years.

Once you're insured, your company can't suddenly cancel your policy. But it can refuse to renew it, so drive carefully!

Homeowner's Insurance

Get a "replacement-cost" policy. It covers the cost of rebuilding your house if it burns to the ground, and increases every year in line with construction costs. "Extended" or "guaranteed" replacement-cost coverage will pay up to 25 percent more than the policy's face value, if that's what it takes to make you whole. For example, if you're insured for $200,000, you could get up to $240,000 to rebuild a home that's a total loss. Your third choice is "actual cash value" coverage. You peg it to the cost of rebuilding your home today, but the company will apply a deduction as the house ages. Inflation will also erode the policy's value, unless you add automatic inflation protection. Cash-value coverage costs less but often leaves you underinsured.

Don't make the mistake of pegging the size of your policy to the resale value of your house. Resale prices include the value of your land, which isn't covered by insurance. A homeowner's policy is for rebuilding or repair after a fire or other damage—an expense that has nothing to do with the price a buyer might offer. Insurance agents or their appraisers will estimate how much coverage you need. If you're not sure whether you're insured for replacement costs, check your policy or call your agent.

Most policies don't cover earthquakes and floods, including water damage from burst pipes and sewer backups. For that, you need a special rider or separate insurance. For an older home, consider "law and ordinance" insurance; if you have to rebuild, it covers the cost of bringing old wiring, foundations, and so on up to code.

Next, you should make an inventory of everything you own. Yes, it's a pain, but it saves you the craziness of having to reconstruct the contents of burned-out rooms if you ever have a major fire. To simplify the job, use a video camera. Record what's in every drawer, every closet, and every room. Talk out loud about everything that's special—furniture, art, china, rugs, furs, jewelry. Keep the disk (or tape) somewhere out of the house—ideally, in a safe-deposit box. You can make the same record with a still camera but it takes longer, especially the notes describing valuable items.

Finally, have your valuables appraised. Your insurance agent can usually give you the names of some professionals, or check the Yellow Pages (for me, the phone book worked much better than the Web). Items of unusual value should be separately insured rather than covered under your general homeowner's policy. You get "scheduled coverage," listing each item and its worth. If anything is damaged, stolen, or lost, the insurer pays its schedule value.

Nevertheless, think carefully about filing claims. You probably think that you've purchased insurance to help cover legitimate losses, but that's not the way insurers think. They simply want to show a profit on your policy. They'll pay your first claim, but if you put in a second they may dump you when it's time to renew. Fair? No, but they hold all the cards.

If you're applying for new insurance, confess to all past claims. There are CLUE reports for personal-property damage, too.

Umbrella Insurance

It covers mega-judgments that exceed the limits of your auto and homeowner's policies. Umbrella insurance doesn't cost a lot and gives you tremendous peace of mind.

LONG-TERM CARE INSURANCE

Long-term care policies help pay the (very high!) nursing home cost if you need constant care. They also cover care in your home or in an adult day-care center, if it's reasonable for you to be there. Here's what you need to know:

- *Should I buy?* There are two reasons to own LTC insurance today: (1) You don't want to use your own savings to pay the enormous nursing home bill. (2) You want to be able to pay for quality care in the private market rather than depending on rickety government programs.

   If you're married, LTC coverage becomes especially important. It protects one spouse from being drained if the other needs full-time care. Under state law, the healthy spouse can retain substantial assets—the house, a car, his or her own income, retirement savings, and part of the ill spouse's property and income. Anything over that amount has to be used toward the nursing home bills. Couples with plenty of money might think they can afford to pay. But an Alzheimer's patient can easily live for a decade or more, at a starting cost of $70,000-plus a year. Don't be shocked at the price—a nursing home is a medical hotel, providing daily room and board as well as maid service, social services, entertainment, and custodial care. Looked at that way, $190 a day isn't out of line.

   If you're single, you don't need insurance if you have enough assets to pay for many years of care and aren't committed to leaving money to your kin.

   If you're middle-income and below, LTC premiums may be higher than you can afford. Save as much money as you can. If you need care, you will probably qualify for government aid.

- *Who will pay if I can't?* If you can't afford care, the government welfare program called Medicaid pays. But nursing homes that cater to Medicaid patients are pretty Spartan. The better places generally want you to pay your own way for at least a year. If you're there longer and run out of assets, you're not kicked out. Medicaid takes over the cost. But the government generally won't pay for a private room, so you'll have to share. If your nursing home closes and you have to go somewhere else, you'll be stuck with Medicaid-only homes, which aren't the greatest.

- *Can I keep my property in the family and still get Medicaid?* Elder-care lawyers will help you give your property away, so you can look "poor" and qualify for Medicaid. It's not illegal but it's unethical and almost certainly unwise. There's no telling what will happen to welfare budgets in the future or how much the taxpayers will be willing to pay for nursing home care. You don't want to depend on it. (It's risky to lose control of your property, too.)

- *When should I buy?* Consider an LTC policy by the time you reach your mid-fifties to mid-sixties. It's cheaper to buy when you're younger, but if you have kids in college, future nursing home care will almost certainly be low on your list. If you wait until your seventies, however, the price soars and your health might not be good enough to qualify for coverage.

- *What should I consider in a policy?* Find out what local nursing homes cost—probably $150 to $250 a day, depending on where you live. An insurance agent will know. Many buyers insure for the full amount. You might also insure for less and pay the difference out of your savings. Add automatic inflation protection so your benefit will keep up with costs. Pick a waiting period before payments kick in: a policy with a six-month wait costs less than one with only a three-month wait. Insure for the longest period of care you can afford, typically three to five years. If you stay longer, you can fall back on personal savings (or Medicaid, if you're out of money). Include home-care coverage, but don't buy a policy that's home-care only. Health failures that require home health aides may force you into a nursing home eventually, and that's the catastrophic cost.

WILLS AND LIVING TRUSTS

A will dictates what will happen to your money and property when you die—and you have one, whether you know it or not. If you never make a personal will, the state steps in and distributes your money according to state law. You might not be happy if you saw the result. If you're single, the law could give your property to your parents rather than your siblings, partner, or a charity you care about. If you're married, your spouse might have to share the assets with your children or other relatives. Some family members might evade the law—triggering a lifetime of ill will. And what if, God forbid, you and your spouse die together in an accident? Relatives might battle over the custody of your kids, not to mention your kids' money. Without a will, you could easily leave your family a mess.

Maybe you think you have a will because you wrote one on your computer, printed it out, and put it in a file. Gong! Not valid in most states. You need the signatures of the right numbers of witnesses, following whatever procedures your state dictates (for example, they might have to sign in front of each other).

Maybe you handwrote your will with no witnesses. It's valid in some states but not in others.

Maybe you videotaped yourself reciting your bequests. That is not a will. The courts will say that you died without one.

You might think that you can skip a will if everything is held jointly or in community property. Such assets normally pass to the other owner, automatically. But there's almost always something you hadn't thought about. Worst case: If you die in an accident that's not your fault, there could be a large financial settlement. The state may appoint an administrator who collects a huge fee, and your family might fight for years over how the money should be split.

You don't want any of this! Make a will!

For speed and ease, a few states provide simple "statutory will" forms you can fill in yourself. You'll also find will-writing kits and software on the Web. But even if you read the instructions carefully, it's all too easy to make a mistake. Muddy wording, for one. If you leave your house to "Sally and the children," do you mean it to be divided equally among them? Or half to Sally and the rest to the children? Or all to Sally, who will take care of the children? That apparently simple bequest could trigger an awful fight. You also could err by not knowing the law. In certain states, for example, anyone who witnesses your will cannot inherit—bad news if you asked a child to sign.

Small errors don't matter, if no one challenges your bequests. But *important, important!* There's one big—and common—mistake that can strip a spouse of assets he or she expected to have. The risk arises from the forms you sign when you buy life insurance, open a bank or investment account, or start an Individual Retirement Account. You're usually asked to name a beneficiary—and that's the person who will inherit, no matter what it says in your will. For example, suppose that when you first started your IRA, you named your sister as beneficiary and forgot about it. Later you married and wrote a will saying, "Give my big fat IRA to my beloved spouse." Sorry, your sister will inherit. The named beneficiary trumps the will. To get her off the IRA, you have to file a new beneficiary form. Do-it-yourselfers may not realize this, or may not remember who their named beneficiaries are.

To simplify the will-writing process and make sure you leave your loved ones safe, see a lawyer—preferably, one who specializes in wills and estates (as usual, ask your friends for recommendations). Simple wills aren't expensive. Start by listing your assets and where you want them to go. Note who officially owns the asset (just you? you and your spouse? you and someone else?), and whether you've named a particular beneficiary. Decide on a guardian for your minor children—who will raise them if you can't? Money left to young children should be held in trust—who should take care of their money and pay their bills until they're on their own? None of this is terribly complicated but it takes some thought. It's interesting, too. An experienced lawyer will raise questions that hadn't occurred to you. He or she will also want to see those beneficiary forms, rather than rely on your memory. If you're married and participate in a company retirement plan, the law says your spouse has to be your beneficiary unless he or she signs a special waiver.

Wills can be changed whenever you want, but not by handwriting a new bequest into your copy. That's invalid. Instead, call a lawyer again, for either a new will or a codicil (supplement) to your current will.

The lawyer will also provide you with a durable power of attorney. That allows someone to manage your money if you become incapacitated.

When you die, your will goes through probate—a legal (mostly clerical) procedure to be sure that the will is valid and the money winds up in the pockets of the people whom you intended to have it. Probate is normally no big deal. The court requires that notice be sent to interested parties to see if they object to the will. If not, it accepts the will as valid and approves the executor (or personal representative) you named. Then comes administration. Creditors are notified, assets valued, taxes paid, and property distributed. Super-simple procedures apply if the estate is small. Some states

even make it easy for your family to handle probate by themselves, if they have the time and interest. In other states, they'll want legal help. They'll probably need an accountant to prepare the estate's tax return.

In a few states (California, for one), the probate process is such a nuisance that lawyers advise you to avoid it. You do so by setting up a living trust and naming a trustee. Like a will, a trust lists your beneficiaries and provides a guardian for your children. But there's no probate or court filing when you die. Instead, your trustee steps in to manage your property and distribute it to heirs. That's especially useful for people who own small businesses, investment real estate, or complicated stocks. While you're alive, you can be your own trustee, managing your money in your usual way. A substitute steps in only if you become incapable. Living trusts are revocable, meaning that you can change the terms (or cancel them) at any time, as long as you're competent.

For the trust to work, however, you have to follow the rules. All your property has to be taken out of your direct name ("John F. Jones") and retitled in your name *as trustee* ("John F. Jones, trustee for the Jones Family Trust dated February 5, 2006"). That takes a lot of paper shuffling. You have to sign all checks as trustee. And you still need a backup will for property that accidentally didn't get into the trust.

A small army of salespeople runs around the country, trying to persuade everyone to buy a living trust (from them, of course!). They tell tall tales about how awful probate is and imply (falsely) that living trusts save taxes in ways that wills can't. They'll sell you bare documents without helping you move your property into the trust (if you don't move the property, the trust is useless). They also imply that probate costs more than establishing a living trust. In fact, either one can cost more, depending on your state and your individual circumstances. Living trusts are more expensive up front (for the trust document and help with retitling the property). Pro-

bate gets more expensive after death (for help with the legal procedures).

If you think you might want a living trust, don't buy from a
salesperson at a seminar. Talk to a lawyer—and not just any old lawyer who does simple wills. You need someone experienced in estate
law, who can help you decide whether a trust is appropriate. In general, trusts may be useful if your assets are complicated, you own
real estate in more than one state, you're rich, or you're well-to-do
and your health is poor. They're generally unnecessary if you're
younger, your assets are modest, or everything will go to a spouse.

For dedicated do-it-yourselfers: Anyone determined to handle
his or her own legal matters can get reliable help through the publi-
cations of Nolo Press at Nolo.com (800-728-3555). You'll find books
and software on preparing wills, living trusts, and many other personal matters.

YOUR LIVING WILL

A living will tells your doctor and your family what you want if
you're permanently unconscious, irreversibly brain-damaged, suffering from dementia, or dying and unable to speak for yourself. Do
you want to be kept alive mechanically, with tubes for food and
water? Or not? If you're comatose and ill, do you want to be treated
with antibiotics to prolong your life? Or not? What if you have
Alzheimer's and no longer know who or where you are? Would you
want to undergo surgery for cancer or heart disease? Or not? These
are the kinds of questions answered by a living will. Without one, a
few states require nourishment to continue for people in permanent comas. That prolongs dying for months, even years. You can
find free living-will forms on the Web through sources such as
Legaldocs.com. The lawyer who does your regular will should include a living will as part of the package.

Important as this document is, however, it's not enough. You also need a health-care proxy or power of attorney for health care. It names someone you trust (plus at least one alternate), to make sure that the terms of your living will are carried out. Otherwise, family members, doctors, hospitals, even strangers opposed to your choice may challenge or ignore your directive. Finally, you need a

A CHECKLIST FOR MAKING CHANGES IN YOUR LIFE

Did you marry or divorce? Change the beneficiary on your life insurance, annuities, and Individual Retirement Account (these go to the named beneficiary, even if your will says something different). Change your will, living trust, power of attorney, and health-care representative. Add or delete your spouse as a covered person on your medical insurance (or get new insurance, if you divorced and lost coverage). Unmarried partners should think about how much they want to protect each other, especially if there are children.

Did you have a new baby or adopt a child? Buy or increase your life insurance, notify your medical insurer, and change your will. If you're responsible for stepchildren, get them into your medical plan. Start saving for college—it's not a moment too soon.

Did your child leave home or leave college? Be sure he or she has health insurance, even if you have to buy it.

Did you move? Write to every institution that holds your assets—bank, broker, mutual fund, insurance company—and change your address. Don't forget your former employers, if you're owed a future income from their pension or retirement-savings plans. Include Social Security, so you'll receive your annual statement of benefits. And notify your auto insurer. Your rates may change, depending on your new address.

Did you change jobs or lose one? Nail down your medical insurance. Replace any life insurance you bought through the company plan. Decide whether to leave your retirement savings in your former company's 401(k) or roll it into an Individual Retirement Account.

Did your spouse die? Review your will, living trust, power of attorney, health-care representative, and IRA or annuity beneficiary. Be sure you have medical insurance (check COBRA coverage if you were covered under your late spouse's plan). Consider whether you still need life insurance.

document authorizing your health-care representative to see your medical records or receive information about your condition. Without it, the doctor or hospital may keep mum because of the medical privacy rules in federal law. How can anyone make decisions about your treatment if the docs aren't allowed to reveal what's wrong?

Your lawyer will prepare your health-care directives, too, or you can get them at Legaldocs.com. And be sure to sit down with your representatives to explain exactly what you want. For help in deepening your thinking, get the free Consumer's Tool Kit for Health Care Decisionmaking at Abanet.org/aging or Caring Conversations at Practicalbioethics.org.

WRITE IT DOWN!

Every time you make a decision about a safety-net product, write it down. Why did you buy that much life insurance, what do you expect it to cover, and for how long? How much disability coverage did you choose? What's the deductible on your medical insurance and is anything excluded from coverage? Maybe you changed your coverage based on something you read here. Maybe you decided that what you already own is right. Either way, summarize your thinking—just a couple of sentences will do—and file it along with the documents it refers to.

Why are summaries important? Because after you've gone through the process of making a big decision, ordinary life takes hold. You'll forget why you made these particular financial choices (everyone does, me included). A year from now, in the dark of some night or after a chat with a salesperson, you might wonder if your safety net is strong enough. The answer is here, in the summaries. You can check in a jiff without having to search the documents (and who wants to bother with that?). When you read Chapter 1, you made a list of all the insurance products you owned. (You did. I know you did). But you weren't always sure whether they really met your needs. Now you know. Anytime you make a change, update these summaries. Then file and forget. When you want them, they'll be here.

A final tip: Go back through this chapter and make a short Action List:

1. Buy more term life insurance if you don't have a policy worth at least eight times your income.
2. Sign up for your company's health-care flexible spending account.
3. If you lack health insurance, find out if there's a catastrophic policy that you can afford. If your young-adult children have no coverage, look into a catastrophic policy for them, too. For younger children, try Insurekidsnow.com.
4. Be sure that your homeowner's policy is for replacement cost.
5. Reshop for auto insurance on the Web.

6. Price long-term care insurance.
7. Write or update a will, a durable power of attorney, and a living will, and name a health-care representative.

Take these steps one at a time. You'll be finished before you know it. Your financial foundation will then be as solid as they come.

5. BUYING A HOUSE

At Last—A Way Through
The Mortgage Maze

Buying a house has gotten to be so *complicated*. Mortgages come in dozens of sizes and shapes, some of them surprisingly risky. Closing costs spread like mold through your checkbook. You turn to the experts to help you find the best deal, but some of them line their pockets at your expense. What should you do? Cut away the wild and crazy stuff that's not worth looking at. Way down deep, mortgages are still simple as long as you let a few good principles be your guide.

While we're at it, the reason for owning a house is simple, too. It's your home in the fullest sense of the word—your private space, your comfort, an achievement that's profoundly satisfying. Erase the thought of a house as a winning lottery ticket, although homeowners sometimes hit the jackpot. Don't even judge it first as an investment. Homeownership is beyond investing—it's a way of life.

People sometimes make good money on their homes, especially during a real-estate boom. But it's no sure thing. History shows only two big booms in the past hundred years. The first one ran for the decade after World War II. The second one started in 1998 and *may* be slowing as I write (you can't predict when booms will end—only that they will).

During normal, *un*boom years, home prices can go anywhere— up, flat, down—depending on the neighborhood and the local economy. Usually, they track the inflation rate, so they rise in dollar terms without adding much to your purchasing power. You might even lose a little, once you subtract the constant cost of upkeep and repair. Homes normally are an especially poor investment compared with the average stock. Between 1980 and mid-2005, the price of the median home rose 1.5 percent a year, adjusted for inflation, while stocks jumped 9.2 percent. But homes have a special value that stocks can't match: They're a place to live. There's nothing like the psychic pleasure of planting your own petunias and unclogging your own drain.

As a homeowner choosing a lifestyle, you have three goals. First, to stay with a mortgage you can afford. Second, to grow your net worth so you can afford to improve your house or trade up to something better. Third, to pay off the mortgage in the end. Homeownership is your best hope of living "free" when you retire. Rent goes on forever. Mortgage payments eventually stop.

With the "personal" in mind, decisions get easier. The best time to buy a home is when you want it, need it, and can afford it, no matter what's happening to housing prices. The best time to sell is when you want to move. The best kind of renovation is one that makes you happy, even if it ends up costing more than you'll get on resale. At the end of this chapter, I'll say a quick word about buying houses for profit. But for your *home*, the investment rules fly out the window. Whatever suits your taste, your budget, and your income expectations, *that's* what you should do.

FALLING IN LOVE WITH HOME EQUITY

Your house can be a wealth builder even in boring real-estate markets, as long as you handle it right. Your objective should be to increase your home equity—that's the difference between your home's market value and the size of your mortgage. If the house is worth $250,000 and you took a $200,000 mortgage, you have $50,000 in equity. The greater your equity, the richer you are.

There are three ways for equity to grow: (1) The magical way, during real estate booms. Home prices rise because eager buyers bid them up. (2) The usual way, for normal times. Home prices stay flat or rise modestly while you lower your mortgage by paying off some of that debt each month. (3) You improve the property in some way. Most homeowners do them all. They pay down their mortgage, modernize or enlarge the house, and hope for some market magic on the side.

There are four ways to lose home equity: (1) Home prices fall. Times have changed and buyers aren't willing to pay as much as you did. (2) You borrow more money against your home by refinancing into a larger mortgage or taking a home-equity loan. (3) You let the property fall into disrepair. (4) Worst case—you run into financial trouble, can't carry the mortgage, and lose the property.

During real-estate booms, people get careless about home equity. They throw it away, by taking home-equity loans and spending the money. Or they choose a mortgage that lets them pay only the interest every month without reducing the principal. "No problem," they think. When they sell the house, they expect to clear enough money to cover their loans *and* provide a down payment on a better place. That can work when real estate is hot. But in normal times, when house prices are flat, you'll have to put money into repaying your mortgage to see your wealth increase.

Boom-time thinking also leads to taking extra investment risk. A favorite strategy is *not* to accumulate home equity. Instead, you keep borrowing against your house and use the proceeds to buy stocks. If the stocks grow faster than the interest you're paying on the loan, your total wealth goes up. You expect to be able to sell the stock whenever you want, pay the tax on your gain, pay off the larger mortgage, and pocket extra cash. Who might this work for?

Someone young who puts all the proceeds into a diversified mutual fund (page 175), holds it faithfully for 15 years or more, and has no trouble carrying the mortgage loan. But everything has to go right. If stocks don't do well or your income is interrupted, this strategy will fail. It's especially risky for people in middle age who might be forced to retire earlier than they thought. If your income drops, it's no fun being stuck with a larger mortgage and having to pray that stocks succeed.

Another investment strategy is to borrow against your house to buy rental property and use the rents to pay the interest on your loan. Who might this work for? Someone with a large enough income to cover the mortgage if tenants are scarce or if the house can't be rented because it's under repair. If you can't pay the mortgage every month without the rents, you're taking too big a risk.

For sleep-tight living, you should always secure your base—and that's your house. Respect your home equity. Cherish it. One thing you want from life is always to feel that your home is safe.

HOW MUCH HOUSE CAN YOU AFFORD?

When you shop for a house, your price range depends on just two things: How big a down payment you make and how much you want to borrow (or can borrow prudently). Add them up and you'll get the maximum you can afford to pay. How much you're able to borrow depends on your income and the size of your existing debt. Lenders have general guidelines they use, although, when home prices are high and credit histories good, they may lend more. Look for yourself on the list below—but remember, "more" isn't always best:

- *If you're a top credit*, with a great credit history, a solid income, and some investments, you can usually spend up to 35 percent of your stable, monthly, gross income on home-owning expenses (principal and interest on your mortgage debt, real-estate taxes, homeowner's insurance, and incidentals such as condominium fees). Up to 50 percent of your income could be committed to total debt, including housing expenses, alimony, child support, and payments toward long-term consumer debt (defined as loans lasting for more than 10 months, including car loans or leases, installment debt, and credit-card debt). If you're self-employed, these ratios apply to your net income after expenses. If you depend on year-end bonuses, part of that bonus might be considered "stable" income.

- *If you're an average credit*, with an acceptable credit history and sufficient income, you can usually spend 25 to 29 percent of your income on basic housing expenses, and 33 to 41 percent for total debt.

- *If you're applying for a special, lower-income loan*, you're allowed up to 33 percent of your monthly income for housing expenses and 38 percent for total debts. For national sources, see page 108. Local banks might have special programs, too.

- *If you want to know whether you can borrow enough to buy a particular house*, ask to be "preapproved" for a mortgage loan. To win preapproval, you fill in an application and have your credit checked. The bank may also verify your income and assets. If you pass, you'll get a letter announcing the maximum you can borrow at current interest rates (and assuming no change in your financial condition). This helps you target a price range for shopping, and gives you an edge over other bidders who haven't yet been approved for a loan. You can get preapprovals from many lenders free on the Web, through a mortgage broker, or from a local lender directly. Some lenders charge for preapprovals and refund the cost if you go through with the loan. But why pay when so many freebies are around?

You can also be "prequalified." That's a free estimate of how large a loan you *might* be able to get, based on your financial data but with no income verification or credit check. Using the Web, you could collect several estimates. Local lenders may prequalify you, too, at no charge. Preapproval, however, is more exact.

- *If you don't want your income checked,* you can ask for a "stated income" loan. That means you don't have to prove what you earn. You state it on your application and your word is considered good. The lender will verify the source of your income and the amount of your assets (your savings and investments), but not the actual size of your paycheck. This can be a great help to people who freelance and don't have actual paystubs. Or maybe you're paying your bills with regular checks from your mother.

  You can also get "stated asset" loans, where you don't have to prove your net worth. You might want to go this route if you're low on savings and are buying the house with a gift from your uncle.

  Frankly, however, these can also be "liar's loans." Are you expecting a raise next month? Liars might pretend they have it now. Do you rely on year-end bonuses? You might pretend you don't. It's illegal to lie to a lender, so these options are dangerous. If you fall behind on payments, the lender may ask for tax returns. Nevertheless, they know you're going "stated" for a reason. They'll charge you an extra quarter-point to half-point in interest to cover their risk, and often want a higher down payment, too. For your own safety, don't engineer a loan that exceeds the income guidelines above.

- *If you buy more house than you really can afford,* the mortgage payments are only part of it. That's not evident, at first. The Devil himself will whisper that, for just a tiny bit more, you can have a mini-manse, with columns, stainless-steel kitchen, and marble floors. But once you move in, you'll also be paying more for heat, electricity, maintenance, and repairs. What's more, you'll face the expense of a wealthier neighborhood, where you'll feel obliged to buy spiffier cars and throw fancy birthday parties for your kids. That's a lot of financial pressure. Your new high style will drain money away from other important things, such as college and retirement investments. So think again. Shop only for houses you can comfortably afford.

- *If you're checking out monthly payments on websites,* keep in mind that that's only part of your total cost. The lenders are showing you only what you'll pay for principal and interest. In addition, you'll owe real-estate taxes and premiums for home-owner's insurance. Those expenses are usually bundled into the amount you pay the lender each month. The lenders hold them in escrow and make the tax and insurance payments for you.

To speed up your house hunting, check the listings on the Web. Go to Realtor.com, type in the towns that interest you, choose some parameters (price, number of bedrooms, garage, fireplace, and so on), then click. You'll find dozens of homes for sale, many with pictures that show you the interior. Also check listings on homes that owners are selling themselves—sites such as Owners.com, Forsalebyowner.com, Assist2sell.com, and Helpusell.com. One more possibility: discount brokerage sites that reward you if you buy a house through them. Ziprealty.com, operating in 10 states and the District of Columbia, rebates 20 percent of the commission it earns from the sale. Realestate.com provides a gift card.

WHAT DO YOU SCORE?

Whether you're a top credit or an average one depends largely on your credit score (page 49). The lowest mortgage interest rates go to borrowers who score above 720. A 700 score is almost as good. As your score drops, rates and fees go up and the amount you're allowed to borrow goes down. Below 620, rates rise a lot and you're offered fewer types of loans. Below 580, you're "subprime," where rates and terms can get really bad. The higher the interest rate you're charged, the less you'll be able to borrow. Your lender will check your credit score as part of your mortgage application and mail you the result.

MORTGAGE 101

Here's a quick run through the words people use when they talk about mortgage loans:

Your *down payment* is the amount of the house price you pay in cash. You borrow the rest. Your loan is *secured* by the value of your house (meaning that the lender can take it, if you don't pay). The amount of money you borrow is the loan's *principal*. The *interest*, expressed as a percentage of the loan amount, is the ongoing price you pay for using the lender's money. On new mortgages, most of each monthly payment goes toward the interest you owe, with only a small amount used to reduce the principal. That reverses toward the end of the loan, when the bulk of each payment reduces the principal.

To *fully amortize* a loan means to pay interest and principal at a rate that will retire the loan in a given number of years. The size of that monthly payment is called the *amortization rate*. (You'd say, "My loan will amortize over 30 years. My amortization rate is $1,200 a month.") If your monthly payments aren't large enough to cover the interest, the loan goes into *negative amortization*. With "negative am," the unpaid interest is added to your loan's principal, so the amount you owe goes up instead of down. (Hot tip—you don't want that to happen.) Need more explanations? You'll find a terrific glossary at Mtgprofessor.com.

HOW BIG A DOWN PAYMENT DO YOU NEED?

Down payments can be large or small. The less you put down, the more limited your borrowing options. Nevertheless, there are mortgages for every pocketbook:

- *When you can put zero or only a flyspeck down.* People with modest incomes, seeking modest homes, can pay as little as 3 percent of the price of the home in cash. Low-down mortgages are usually made through special programs offered by lenders all over the country. Some are insured by the Federal Housing Administration. (For leads to FHA lenders, go to Hud.gov, click on "Search," then on "Lenders.") Or they might be sponsored by housing-finance corporations such as Fannie Mae (at Fanniemae.com, click on "Find a Lender Search"). Veterans can put zero down on loans guaranteed by the U.S. Department of Veterans Affairs, regardless of the size of their incomes (go to HomeLoans.va.gov for information and a list of VA-approved lenders). Borrowers with high incomes and assets, and willing to pay a higher-than-normal interest rate, might also be able to buy with nothing down. Mortgage brokers (page 118) are the experts on low down-payment plans.
- *When you can pay more than a flyspeck but not a lot.* Lenders normally let you put as little as 5 percent down, as long as you have enough income to carry the monthly payments. Check the interest rate and fees at the many places that will lend to you online. Three good possibilities: Eloan.com, Indymac.com, and Mortgage.com.

Lenders charge a higher interest rate for a low-down loan (that's for down payments under 20 percent). Your house will cost you more because you're borrowing more money more expensively.

Your bank also may require you to buy mortgage insurance, to protect its loan if you default. By law, lenders have to cancel this coverage automatically, once your equity in your home reaches 22 percent of the price you originally paid. On mortgages sold to Fannie Mae or a similar group called Freddie Mac (as most are), you can request that the coverage be canceled if your equity has reached 20 percent of the home's current value and you've held the loan for at least five years.

Sometimes, the lender buys the mortgage insurance and wraps the cost of the premiums into the loan. That makes them tax-deductible (they'll be treated as mortgage interest). Alternatively, the lender might skip the insurance and give you the mortgage in two parts—a first mortgage for 80 percent of the cost of the house, at regular rates, and a second, "piggyback" mortgage for the rest of the money, at a higher rate. If you plan to hold the mortgage for a long time, however, you might be better off with separate mortgage insurance. You'll be able to drop it eventually, which will cut your costs. (You also can get rid of the piggyback early, by accelerating payments.)

- *When you can put at least 20 percent down.* You have a wider choice of loan terms, including loans with lower rates. And you don't need mortgage insurance.
- *When you can choose how much to put down.*
  1. *Choose a larger down payment* if you want a loan with a lower interest rate and better terms; if you want to be mortgage-free by the time you retire; if your income is irregular and you're safer with lower monthly payments; or if you'd otherwise fritter your spare money away.

2. *Choose a smaller down payment* if you're short of cash to move; if you owe credit-card debt and will use the extra money to pay if off; and if you can make the higher monthly mortgage payments without killing yourself (you have to take a larger loan when you put less money down).

How about choosing a smaller down payment so that you can invest the rest of your money somewhere else? Not a good idea. The cost of this choice is far higher than people realize. That's because lenders charge higher interest rates and fees to people who put less money down. To make up for that extra out-of-pocket cost, the cash return on your outside investment has to be surprisingly large—typically, equal to your higher mortgage rate plus about 5 percent. Say, for example, that you could have borrowed at 6 percent but your lower down payment raised your rate to 6.25 percent (plus higher fees). To make up for that extra 0.25 percent (applied to your entire loan) the amount you invested would have to earn about 11.25 percent, and that's just to break even! You need an even higher return to make a profit.

Skimping on your down payment almost never makes sense. An investment in your mortgage when you buy your house is one of the smartest ways you can use your money.

THE MAJOR MORTGAGE TYPES

Fixed-Rate Mortgage

Fixed rates are safest, from a budget point of view. Your monthly payments are set for as long as you hold the loan.

Choose a fixed-rate loan if you think interest rates are unusually low. Or you want to lock in your mortgage payments, for budget reasons. Or you'd go crazy with worry when interest rates went up.

Adjustable-Rate Mortgage (ARM)

ARMS are cheaper at the start. You get a low, bargain interest rate that's good for one month to several years, depending on the loan. Monthly payments start low, too. When the bargain period ends, your rate will rise to the level of the general market. From that point, your payments could rise or fall every 6 to 12 months.

The general market is measured by an "index," which averages a range of interest rates. There are many, many types of indexes. Your bank will probably use one of the following four: The CODI—follows the interest rates that banks pay on three-month certificates of deposit. A Treasury index—follows the rates that the government pays on various Treasury securities. The COFI—follows the rates that savings institutions in Arizona, California, and Nevada pay for funds. The LIBOR—follows the rates that London banks pay for U.S. dollars. In practical terms, it doesn't really matter which index your lender uses—you'll take whatever it offers. LIBOR rises and falls more rapidly than the other indexes do.

When adjusting your ARM rate, the bank takes the index it uses and adds a fixed number of percentage points called a *margin*. To see how this works, assume that your margin is 2.5 points. With the Treasury index at 3 percent, plus a 2.5 margin, your interest rate comes to 5.5 percent. If Treasuries rise to 4 percent, adding the margin raises your rate to 6.5 percent. Borrowers with good credit get a low margin over the index (2.25 points is very good). Borrowers with poorer credit pay a higher margin (3 points or more).

Your mortgage payments can't rise to the sky even if interest rates soar. There are *caps* on the loan that establish the most you'd ever have to pay. On most ARMs, rate can't rise by more than 2 percentage points a year or 6 percentage points over the life of the loan. To get a feel for whether the ARM could become a strain, ask the lender to show you what happens to payments in the worst case.

Choose an ARM if you need a low initial rate to buy the house you want. Or you have a high income (or expect it to rise) and are sure you can handle higher payments when they come. Or you'll own the house for only four or five years, which is when you reap the surest savings with ARMs. In general, ARMs have been cheaper over the long run, for people who don't mind fluctuating payments.

Hybrid ARM

With this type of ARM your interest rate is fixed for the first 3, 5, 7, or 10 years. Then you switch to a variable rate, which usually adjusts every year. The longer the fixed-rate period, the higher your initial rate will be. The first time it adjusts, it could jump by as much as 5 percentage points. Lenders refer to hybrids in shorthand. On the Web, a loan labeled "5/1" gives you a fixed rate for 5 years, then a variable rate that changes every year. A "7/1" loan fixes your rate for seven years, then changes every year.

Choose a hybrid if you want a lower fixed rate for the first few years and expect to be able to handle variable rates after that. It's also good for people who expect to sell within the fixed-rate period.

Interest-Only Mortgage (IO)

For the first few years of an IO mortgage, you pay only the interest on your loan and nothing toward principal. That gives you lower monthly payments but you're not reducing the debt. After 3 to 10 years (you choose), your payments jump to a level high enough to retire the loan over its remaining term. For example, say you take a 30-year loan and pay nothing toward principal for the first five years. In the sixth year, you have to start paying enough to retire the loan over the remaining 25 years. That's called *recasting* the loan. Your monthly payment could jump by 30 percent to 50 percent.

Beware the ads for IO mortgages showing that they're cheaper than other loans. They're not. Banks like to compare them with fixed-rate loans, where they do indeed look lower-cost. But that's deceptive and the banks know it. An IO is usually an adjustable-rate loan. It should be compared with an equivalent ARM minus the interest-only option. That will show that an IO costs more, due to a higher interest rate.

Choose an IO loan—hardly ever. Consider it only if you really need the lowest possible monthly payments to qualify for a house you want. You're gambling that you can handle the basic loan (which will be a large one, relative to your income) and make sharply higher payments when the time rolls around. IOs *always* cost more in interest, whether you hold them for 5 years or 30 years, both because of the higher rate and because the loan principal stays high.

Option ARM, FlexPay ARM, Pick-A-Pay

These are fancy names for a fancy, complicated, and—to my mind—dangerous new mortgage. Trust me, you don't want it. Don't even bother reading this section unless you're tempted.

With an Option ARM, borrowers can choose the amount they pay each month. You're offered the following four choices: (1) the loan's minimum payment, which is less than the interest owed; (2) a payment large enough to cover the interest; (3) a payment large enough to retire the loan on a 15-year schedule; or (4) a payment large enough to retire the loan over 30 years. If you're tight on money, all these options sound just great. In a month when you have a lot of bills, you can pay the minimum on your mortgage and (maybe) catch up later. But when you pay less than the interest owed, the bank adds the unpaid interest to your total debt. That's "negative amortization"—where the size of your loan goes up instead of down. Negative "am" gets you further into debt.

What's more, Option ARMs are often marketed deceptively. They're advertised at a super-low "teaser" rate, maybe 1.5 percent. Your payments are based on that tiny rate for the whole first year. But here's the trick: The teaser rate lasts only for the loan's *first month!* In the second month, you start owing the regular, higher interest rate—maybe 6 percent. Your teaser payments aren't high enough to cover all the interest due. Whammo, negative am again—your mortgage debt is going up. Did your banker tell you that?

In the second year of an Option ARM, your minimum monthly payments can rise by no more than 7.5 percent. That still may be less than you need to cover the ongoing interest on the loan! If you stick with the minimum (fatally easy, when so many other bills are due), you'll run up your debt even more. It gets harder and harder to catch up.

The "optional"—or flexible-payment—part of your loan usually runs for five years. After that, your monthly payments jump, jump, jump. You'll have to start paying enough to retire the loan over its remaining term. The amount could be huge, especially if interest rates have risen.

Being clever, you might say, "Hey, I can pay the minimum for five years before the trouble starts. By then, I'll have sold the house." Ha. Who can outwit a bank? If your minimum payments lead to a lot of negative am—enough so that the loan amount rises by 10 percent (sometimes 25 percent)—the bank will take away your right to choose. You'll be forced, right then, to start making monthly payments high enough to retire the loan. The bank will only yawn if you say you can't afford it.

If you do sell the house, pray that it has risen enough in value to cover your original loan, *plus* any additional debt you ran up by making minimum payments, *plus* the 5 percent or 6 percent commission you'll have to pay the real estate agent, *plus* the amount of your down payment, *plus* your closing costs. That's what you'll need to break even on this "investment." Anything less, and you'll lose money. If the house has dropped in value, you may owe the lender more than you can sell it for.

Choose an Option ARM—never. They're too tempting, by far, for buyers squeezing to get a house. You'll keep finding reasons to pay only the minimum, the size of your debt will rise, and you may be socked with higher payments when you least expect it. Reading the ads for these loans makes me mad. Lenders dangle all the other things you can "afford" to do when you're making minimum mortgage payments, such as buying furniture or taking a vacation. Sure—and meanwhile they're making money from all the extra interest you're paying on your Option ARM. I wouldn't even have mentioned these loans if they weren't being so widely pushed. Among their many other sins, they're complicated. In the money business, "complicated" means "they win, you lose." Cheap and simple is *always* best.

PAYING POINTS

When you borrow money to buy a house, the lender charges you not only interest but also *points*. A point is 1 percentage point of the loan amount. That's $1,000 for every $100,000 you borrow. You can pay in cash or add the cost of the points to your mortgage loan. The more points you pay, the lower your mortgage interest rate. Lower rates mean lower monthly payments. So what should you do—cut your interest rate by paying extra points, or not? Here's how to decide:

- *Pay zero or minimal points* if you'll be in the house for only a few years. Additional points would cost you more than the extra interest you'll save.
- *Pay extra points* if you'll hold the house for many years. Over the long run, a lower interest rate will save you money.
- *To compare the dollars and cents,* Web calculators help. At Dinkytown.net, see whether it pays to use extra cash to lower your points or to raise your down payment. At Mtgprofessor .com and Choosetosave.org, see how long it takes for the money you save by getting a lower interest rate to offset the cost of paying higher points.

YOUR MORTGAGE TERM

When you take out a mortgage, how long a term do you want? The answer depends on the monthly payments you can afford.

- *A traditional, 30-year mortgage* carries low monthly payments. It's the right loan for first-home buyers and people with young families. Your debt declines slowly during the first 10 years because most of your payment goes toward interest. But it's usually the only (or best!) loan for a tight budget.
- *A 15-year mortgage* appeals to people at a different stage of life. You're middle-aged (the *new* middle age—50, not 40!), earning more money than you used to, and with the word "retirement" getting a little more real. Short-term mortgages are huge money savers. Monthly payments are higher, but you get a lower interest rate and retire the loan over fewer years. That can put tens of thousands of dollars into your pocket, thanks to the interest you save. You can also get loans for 10-year and 20-year terms. I like short-term loans for younger people, too, if they can handle the monthly payments.

- *The new 40-year mortgages* offer especially low payments to the cash-poor. They're more predictable than interest-only loans. You won't face a sudden jump in payments five years from now, the way IO borrowers will. The downside (and it's a big one): You pay a high rate. When you sell, you'll have paid much more interest and built less equity than with a 30-year loan.

SHOULD YOU LOCK?

When the bank agrees to lend you money, the interest rate isn't guaranteed. You'll get the going rate when the loan is closed (and the bank might squeeze you for more). If you hate uncertainty, you can *lock* today's rate—paying the lender a fee to guarantee it for 30 to 60 days. You never can tell what will happen to rates from week to week. They bounce around, even in the midst of a falling or rising trend. If you're at the very edge of your borrowing capacity, you'd be wise to lock so that the loan doesn't get away from you.

CUT YOUR DEBT! PREPAY YOUR LOAN!

You *prepay* a mortgage when you make a larger monthly payment than the bank requires. You can do it by raising the dollar amount you pay each month or by putting a slug of cash toward the mortgage all at once. Any extra payment reduces the size of the loan. That does two splendid things: It lowers the amount of interest you have to pay and builds your home equity faster. If you stay in the house, you will burn the mortgage sooner. If you sell, you'll have more equity to put toward the next house you buy.

Prepaying a mortgage is an *investment* and I can tell you exactly what the return on that investment will be. Your gain is always the same as the interest rate you pay. If you have a 6 percent mortgage, you earn 6 percent on every prepayment you make. Let me give you an example, to show you why:

Say you have a 6 percent mortgage and put in an extra $1,000. Your mortgage principal drops by $1,000, so you're no longer paying interest on that amount. At 6 percent on $1,000, you're saving $60 cash—a 6 percent return on your money.

The same will be true with any other interest rate. If you make a prepayment on a 7 percent loan, you'll earn 7 percent on your money, and so on and so forth. The return is built-in; it's guaranteed. You can compare it directly with the yields available on other safe investments, such as bank certificates of deposit.

Here's when it's a good idea to prepay:

1. *In middle age.* It's smart to own your home, free and clear, by the time you retire and your regular paychecks stop. At that stage of life, you'll want the lowest possible expense.
2. *In a flat housing market.* By prepaying, you build equity faster so you can move up to a better house.
3. *If you inherit a bucket of money.* Prepaying a mortgage slashes your cost of living.
4. *If prepayment looks like a good investment.* For the conservative part of your investment pot, prepaying a mortgage may be a better deal than a bank account or bond mutual fund. In a pinch, you can borrow the money back by using a home-equity line of credit.
5. *To shorten a long-term mortgage.* For flexibility, you might have taken a 30-year or even 40-year loan. Prepayments will help you build equity faster. That extra equity helps you trade up to a better house.
6. *If you just hate debt.* 'Nuff said.

The automated way to prepay: Add a fixed number of dollars— say, $50 or $100—to your regular monthly payments. Automate the payments, so you don't notice them. On fixed-rate loans, extra payments instantly reduce the term. With ARMs, the lender keeps the same term but reduces the monthly payments you owe. Ignore the reduction. Keep to the higher level of payments and the mortgage will shorten itself. You may think prepayments don't matter if you expect to sell the house in just a few years. But they do. No matter when you sell, prepayments cut your total interest cost and increase your equity.

Should you buy a biweekly payment plan? No, don't. These plans arrange to pay half your monthly mortgage every two weeks. Because of the way the calendar runs, you wind up paying for one extra month a year. On a 30-year loan, for example, biweekly payments shorten the term to about 23 years and save you interest no matter when you sell your house—so that part is fine. But commercial plans cost $195 to $350 and they're just as easy to do yourself. Here's Jane's Biweekly Payment Plan, free of charge: Add one-twelfth of a payment to the regular amount you pay each month.

How much will you save? Play with the calculators at Bank rate.com, Choosetosave.org, Dinkytown.net, or Mtgprofessor.com. They'll calculate the savings from any prepayment schedule. Or download the free Home Buyer's Calculator Suite from Hsh.com. I promise you that the result of prepaying will amaze you.

Are there penalties for prepaying? Most mortgages don't impose any prepayment penalties. Where they exist, they're on loans with especially low fees or low initial interest rates. You might even have accepted a penalty deliberately when you took the loan, in return for a lower interest rate. You won't be penalized for using the prepayment strategies I've been discussing here. (Check your mortgage agreement or ask your bank if you're in doubt.) Where penalties exist, they usually apply only during the loan's first three to five years, and only if you refinance (page 121) or prepay more than 20 percent of the loan balance in a single year. Penalties may be stiffer on loans to people with poor credit scores.

Are you keeping your big mortgage because you "need" the tax deductions? Phooey. "Needing" deductions must be the most successful piece of financial propaganda that the industry has ever launched. Okay, you can tax-deduct mortgage interest. But your tax savings amount to only a fraction of the cost. You pay the rest right out of your pocket—money transferred from you to the bank. If you're in the 25 percent bracket, the write-off saves you 25 cents out of every dollar you pay in interest; the remaining 75 cents is pure expense. If you had no mortgage (or a smaller mortgage), guess what would happen to every dollar you *didn't* pay in interest? The government would get 25 cents; the remaining 75 cents would be yours to keep. Getting rid of a loan is pure gain.

Some borrowers should not prepay. In the big picture, other things come first. Contribute to your retirement plan. Pay off consumer debt. Build a Cushion Fund, for ready cash. Pay off home-equity loans (page 44) that carry higher interest rates than the basic mortgage does. If you have children, contribute to a college savings plan. *Then* put extra money toward reducing your housing costs.

HOW TO FIND A GOOD MORTGAGE

Start with the Web. Check rates at the three sites I mentioned on page 105. Ignore their "Wow!" offers for interest-only ARMs and Option ARMs (the loans that let the banks rake in extra interest while you pay, pay, pay). Instead, scope out their plain-vanilla ARMs and fixed-rate loans. Rates and fees are often the best you'll find anywhere. The more questions the lender asks you, the more accurate the rate quote is likely to be. There's no problem borrowing by Web. E-lenders are fully equipped to handle their side of the paperwork, by phone, e-mail, and local agents. That is, if your credit is good. If it's poor, you'll need special underwriting.

Ask your bank. You might prefer the experience of talking with someone locally. But go this route only if you get the same low interest rate and fees you find online. After an opening conversation with your friendly banker Bob, you'll deal by phone and e-mail anyway. Once the loan closes, the bank will probably sell it to an investor somewhere else in the U.S. (or the world), so you get no particular advantage from borrowing in your hometown.

Ask a mortgage broker. Mortgage brokers know all the lenders and the offers. Their job is to shop the market and find you a suitable loan at the lowest possible rate. They can be especially helpful if you're a first-time buyer, need an FHA or VA loan, have problem credit, can't document your income, or need other special services. Unfortunately, not all mortgage brokers play fair. Some of them overcharge, in ways you don't suspect.

Getting a loan through a mortgage broker should cost exactly the same as if you went to the lender yourself. But some of them overcharge in ways you don't suspect. For example, they might: (1) Steer you into a higher-rate loan because it pays them a higher commission, all the time telling you that it's the best you can get. (2) Quote you an extra-low rate (even lower than you found on the Web) to get your business, then tell you (falsely) "the market has changed" and deliver a higher rate. (3) Say they're charging you "one point" (1 percent of the loan) without disclosing that the lender pays them a second point, which is included in your mortgage rate. (4) Claim "our services are free," then put you into a high-rate loan that pays them an extra-high commission. *No* services are free.

To be sure you're dealing with an honest broker, start by negotiating a fee. Then ask to see—actually *see*—the sheet that shows the wholesale interest rate and points the lender charges. The sheet might say "6 + 1," meaning 6 percent plus one point. You should pay that amount plus the broker's fee, no more. The broker should put the fee in writing and agree not to add a percentage to any third-party charge, such as the appraisal.

Consider doing business with one of the people who call themselves an Upfront Mortgage Broker. They promise to find you the best wholesale rate you qualify for and to disclose all their fees—both what you pay and the fees they receive from the lender. You'll find them listed at Mtgprofessor.com. If none are local, you can deal with some of them by phone or online. For other mortgage brokers, check the National Association of Mortgage Brokers (Namb.org), the Yellow Pages, real-estate agents, and friends. Ask the brokers to follow the same procedures that Upfront Mortgage Brokers do. If they won't, don't work with them.

Ask your real-estate agent. He or she may know of a local lender with good deals. But back off, if the real-estate firm has an affiliated mortgage company. Your agent might pressure you to pop over to the next desk and apply for a loan. Don't sign anything until you've shopped around, to find out what rates and fees are normal for someone in your situation. The mortgage you're being pushed toward might be high-priced.

Go to a lender directly—a mortgage company, bank, savings and loan, or credit union. But apply only after you've checked the Web to be sure the offer is competitive.

Apply through several sources—a bank, a mortgage broker, a Web lender—to see what you can get. Shop, shop, shop! Half a percentage point saved on a 30-year, $200,000 loan is worth almost $64 a month. Multiple mortgage applications normally show on your credit history and pull down your credit score. But all applications made within a single 14-day period count as a single application, so you're okay.

Don't answer spam ads for low-rate mortgages. They aren't from real lenders. At best, the spammers are collecting personal information to sell to middlemen who, in turn, will sell it to real lenders, who may want to offer you a loan. At worst, they'll use your information in some identity-theft scam.

WATCH OUT FOR THE FEE MONSTER

Some lenders go crazy with fees and mortgage-closing costs because they know that consumers usually don't compare. The same $200,000 loan could cost anywhere from $2,000 to $10,000, depending on where you borrow. So shop for fees as well as rates. You want to be sure that an apparently low-rate loan doesn't come larded with extra costs. A typical list of lender fees includes points, "origination fee" (an additional percentage point for making the loan), underwriting, document preparation, escrow, recording, wire transfer, lender inspection, payments to the bank's lawyer, rate lock, courier, "processing" (a shameless kitchen-sink fee), pizza, coffee, Gucci shoes (well, maybe not, but if they could . . .). You also pay for the credit report, appraisal, and title insurance.

Lenders have to give you a "good-faith estimate" of their fees within three days of receiving your loan application. But an estimate isn't a guarantee. At the closing itself (or only twenty-four hours before), you might discover that fees have miraculously risen. At that point, all you can do is walk away or pay.

Web lenders are starting to bundle their fees into a single charge and guarantee it—a welcome development. Wherever consumers are able to make comparisons, fees soon decline. You'll also find some lenders who advertise that they have "no closing costs"; they've bundled those costs into the mortgage, which probably carries a slightly higher interest rate. I like these loans because there's just one number to compare—the rate—with nothing else to trip you up.

At the closing, you'll also have other costs, such as local transaction taxes, prepaid interest if your mortgage closes before the end of the month, and the price of any oil or propane that the seller left in the tank. You'll also owe "impounds"—your first monthly payments toward real-estate taxes and homeowner's insurance. Some lenders let you pay your taxes and insurance separately, but may charge you for the privilege.

WHEN TO REFINANCE

To *refinance* means taking a new loan against your home and using the proceeds to pay off the old one. You'd make the exchange if you can get a lower interest rate. You might also get a lower monthly payment, a more appropriate mortgage, a shorter payoff period, or a cash loan against your home equity.

You cannot save money by switching into a loan with a higher interest rate. It can be made to *look* cheaper. The lender can stretch out the term of the loan, to give you lower monthly payments. But it's all baloney. Higher-rate loans still cost you more.

Even a lower-rate loan can cost you more, in dollars, if you stretch out the term. For example, say that you took a 30-year mortgage six years ago, so today you have 24 years left to pay. If you refinance ("refi") into a new 30-year loan, you're stretching out your remaining principal payments for an extra six years. That's an extra six years of interest costs—not cheap.

You might think that refinancing into a longer-term loan doesn't matter because you won't keep it for 30 years. But it matters a lot. Ask the bank to show you how much interest you'd pay, on both the old loan and the new one, if you sold the house after, say, seven years. You might be surprised to see that the new loan doesn't save you as much as you thought.

If the bank doesn't let you refinance over exactly the number of years remaining on your old loan, go for the first available shorter term—say, 20 years. There's another option: Take the longer-term loan but turn it into a shorter one. A 30-year loan can become a 24-year loan if you simply make slightly higher payments every month. Use a mortgage calculator (page 116) to check this out.

Lenders typically charge the same fees for refinancing a mortgage as they do for issuing new ones. They're delighted to fold those costs right into the loan, so you're borrowing more. You'll also see "no-cost" refis, which carry a slightly higher interest rate (the costs are contained in the rate, rather than being listed separately). A "no-cost" might be cheaper if you plan to move pretty soon. But if you'll probably stay in the house for five years or more, it's best to take a lower-rate refi and pay the closing costs in cash.

When looking for refinancing, check the Web to see what's available. Then go to your current lender (the place where you send the mortgage payment) and ask it to beat the best price that you've found elsewhere.

Should you do a cash-out refinancing? With a cash-out, you take a larger loan than you had before. You pay off the old mortgage and use the extra money for other things. The interest rate on a cash-out is a little higher than on a straight refinancing, and the larger loan reduces your home equity. So you're incurring extra costs and spending down your wealth. The question becomes, what you're spending the money on:

- *A new kitchen?* The down payment on a second home? A child's tuition? These are reasonable choices, provided that you can make the larger mortgage payments without strain.
- *Starting a business?* Have a fallback plan to protect your home if the business doesn't work.
- *Investing in stock?* You're trading a pretty secure investment for a riskier one, probably on a stockbroker's promise that, over

the long term, you can't lose. You *can* lose. I like the stock market just fine (Chapter 7), but invest with money you've saved on the side, not with your home equity.

- *Taking a really great vacation?* Please, no. You'll be paying for that vacation for the next 30 years.
- *Paying off your credit cards?* Okay, but only if you'll push yourself to prepay this portion of the loan, and only if you know you won't run up consumer debt again.

What if you need cash-out money but mortgage interest rates have gone up? Turn to a smaller second mortgage or home-equity line. They'll cost you less than refinancing the mortgage you have.

WHEN YOU SELL

You don't have to pay the traditional 5 or 6 percent real estate commission. That's what the real-estate broker quotes (sometimes even 7 percent). But many of them will negotiate. Brokers who stick to the higher commission will probably tell you they're worth every penny because they can get you more for your home. But there's no proof of that (it's like stockbrokers saying they'll find you stocks that go up). Plenty of fine and experienced brokers will take your listing for less and put the same effort into selling your house that the pricier ones do.

On the Web, you'll find discount brokers who will sell your house for as little as 4 percent or even 3 percent. That's a saving of $7,000 to $10,500 on a $350,000 house. Some traditional brokers boycott the discounters and won't show the houses they list—proof that they care more about protecting their incomes than helping their customers find homes. But the discount business is growing because home sellers want it and the discounters advertise widely enough to attract clients. Check sites such as Ziprealty.com,

Helpusell.com, Foxtons.com, and Assist2sell.com. They're not in all states, but may be in yours. To see if there's an independent discounter nearby, enter words such as "discount real estate broker" or "4 percent real estate commission" in your Web search engine. Almost certainly, someone will turn up.

How about selling the house yourself, without a broker? It's easier in a hot market than a cool one but works anytime for sellers willing to make the effort. On a $350,000 house, you'd save $21,000—a payoff worth working for. You don't have to put your own hand-lettered sign in the window. Web sites such as Owners .com and Forsalebyowner.com sell professional For Sale yard signs, an 800 number for receiving calls, and a listing on their own website (with pictures of your house). In most cities, you also get a listing on the Multiple Listing Service (MLS) that all real-estate brokers use. From the MLS, listings migrate to Realtor.com—a big break for do-it-yourselfers. People looking for homes nationwide tap into Realtor.com, where your house can be seen along with the houses shown by brokers. There's pots of free info on the Web about pricing your house, preparing it for sale, and negotiating terms. If it doesn't sell, you can always try a broker later.

FOR MORE INFORMATION

If you need more details, check out two websites: Mtgprofessor .com and Hsh.com. You could spend half a day reading their articles and advice. HSH also publishes a *Homebuyer's Mortgage Kit*, at this writing, $23 from HSH Associates, Dept. HMK, 237 West Parkway, Pompton Plains, NJ 07444; 800-873-2837. Besides advice, the kit gives you current mortgage rates and terms from lenders in your area. Jack Guttentag (the "mtgprofessor") has a book called *The Mortgage Encyclopedia* ($19.95, published by McGraw-Hill). It's got tons of detailed mortgage information and good consumer advice, plus eye-opening sections on how you can be skinned by lenders and mortgage brokers.

ARE YOU SURE YOU WANT TO INVEST IN REAL ESTATE?

The rules for investing in residential real estate are completely different from the rules for buying your own home. The house you'd buy for the rental trade may not be one you'd like to live in—it's probably smaller and without as many amenities. It may be in a neighborhood that otherwise doesn't appeal to you. You shouldn't spend a lot of money fixing it up—just the necessities. The fancier you get, the less profitable the investment is going to be. Some investors prefer to buy "starter" houses in new subdivisions.

Ideally, you want your rents to cover all your expenses plus at least 5 percent. In today's market, however, that's almost impossible. Home prices are too high and rents too low. Hopeful investors are dipping into their personal incomes and savings to cover costs, trusting that they'll eventually sell at a large enough profit to make it worthwhile. You can luck out, when homes are hot. When prices cool, however, you'll get subpar returns (maybe even negative returns) from a rental property that can't pay for itself.

Rental real-estate investing is different from home owning in another way: It's a small business that you have to learn to run efficiently. Successful entrepreneurs look at dozens, even hundreds, of properties to find the few that work. They nail all the costs—not just mortgage, taxes, and insurance, but also advertising for tenants, repairs, utilities, maintenance, reserves for repainting and replacements, fix-up costs when a renter leaves, and dozens of others. They maintain a line of credit to carry the property through a bad rental market or a period when it's out of commission for repairs.

Most important—you need the temperament to be a landlord.

Can you put up with complaining tenants? Are you willing to be called at midnight to fix a faucet? Can you threaten to evict if the rent comes late? Can you actually evict—even a "friend" who has fallen on hard times? Even a single mom? With a puppy? If not, you'll be running a charity. Better not put your money there.

Alternatively, you might try to find a run-down property, fix it up quickly, and "flip" it to a new owner at a higher price. For that, you need a really hot market to succeed. Everyone else is looking for that flipper fixer-upper, too. In normal markets, it's hard to make money after costs.

Real estate can be profitable as long as you understand that it's a business, not a hobby or a get-rich-quick game. Before even starting, bone up on the principles. My favorite guides are *How to Get Started in Real Estate Investment* ($29.95) and *How to Manage Residential Property for Maximum Cash Flow and Resale Value* ($39.95), by John Reed, available only through his website at John-treed.com. Reed also has a terrific Web page called Real Estate Guru Ratings, evaluating the books and real-estate seminars on the market. Don't miss it. If you're interested in investing, this will steer you to good guys and away from the many charlatans in the game.

INVESTING IN A VACATION HOME

The rules for buying a second home are just like the rules for buying your first one. You want to be able to cover the mortgage without strain. If you plan to rent the house when you're not there, you'll need a good local agent to keep it in shape. Desirable rental properties are near beaches, lakes, ski slopes, and other destinations, not in the middle of nowhere. They're well kept and suitable for families. You'll almost never get enough rent to cover your costs, but any rents lower your expense. Think of your "guests" as helping you own your getaway dream house at a discount.

YOUR CHECKLIST

There's a lot in this chapter, but ultimately homebuyers have to make only a few decisions. What can you spend on a house without wiping yourself out? On your mortgage, do you want a fixed rate or an adjustable rate? Are you getting the lowest rates and fees for the loan you want? And finally, will you be happy there? With luck, your house will turn out to be a fine investment, but most of all it should be a home you love.

6. PAYING FOR COLLEGE

College! Yikes!
No Way Can I Save That Much

It's funny, about college for kids. The cost sounds appalling. You can't imagine paying the bills. You start an education fund and think, "What a joke." Or you think, "The kids are small, I've got plenty of time." Then, in a blink, they're off to school. Somehow, all the checks get written and, like every other parent, you survive.

Here's how the college-money game usually plays out: You save some money toward the cost (one-third would be nice; starting early makes it work). Your child saves money, too, from his or her paychecks and holiday gifts. Depending on your income and the school you choose, you might get a government grant or a tuition discount. When enrollment rolls around, your student gets government-subsidized student loans. You pay the rest out of current earnings—yours and whatever your child can add. The total, from all these sources, tells you which school you can afford. Don't—please don't—plan on taking loans yourself. You won't want to carry a pile of extra debt into your retirement years. Your kids have plenty of time to repay education loans. You don't.

When judging college by cost, keep telling yourself this: More isn't better. Brand-name colleges raise prices to the sky because brand-besotted parents equate cost with quality. But many lower-cost schools will provide an equally good—sometimes better—program for your child. Kids make what they can of their chances, and usually fall in love with whatever college they attend (that's the weekend-party bond). Of my brood, two went to small private colleges of midrange cost; one went to a large private university; two went to a state university. All got the education they wanted and graduated into life.

YEAH, BUT HOW MUCH?

Avert your eyes from projections that show Yale costing $23 zillion in 15 years. So what if it does? Private, *un*Yales cost one-third less, and offer substantial grants and tuition discounts. Some 80 percent of America's students go to public colleges and universities at less than half the private-college price. In fact, of all full-time students, a majority pays less than $6,000 in tuition and fees. You'll find honors programs everywhere for the super-smart. As for the kids who will major in beer, you don't want to pay top dollar anyway. If Yale sticks in your mind, well, your income and assets will also go up, over 15 years. It will be no harder to pay tuition in the future than it is today.

In other words, you don't have to panic. But if you have children and haven't yet started on college savings, get going ASAP. The earlier you budget the money, the easier saving is going to be. You'll build those monthly deposits right into your lifestyle, which means you'll hardly notice them at all. If you're saving already, save more. To make it easier, follow these steps:

1. Earmark a special college-savings account, where you can see the money build.

2. Establish a specific savings goal and contribute the same, fixed amount out of every paycheck.
3. Make the savings automatic (where have you heard that before?)—straight out of your bank account.
4. Raise your contribution to college savings every year.
5. Save any windfalls, such as birthday money or unexpected bits of income.
6. Redirect income that you've been spending on something else. For example, if you finish paying off a credit card, switch those regular payments into college savings.

When estimating how much to save, assume that the cost of college will be about the same in the future as it is today, relative to your resources. Start with the table on the next page, which shows the average prices in 2005–2006, or check the actual cost of a particular school you like. Few parents save the whole sum, but you can aim at one of two target amounts:

- *Save "enough to get over the hump,"* so you can feel sure that the rest of the money can be raised from earnings and student loans. Typically, that's one-third of today's total four-year college cost (and more, if your income is higher than average).
- *Save the minimum dollar amount that the schools will require you to pay*—called the Expected Family Contribution, discussed below.

To estimate how much you'll have to save each month, use the calculators at Collegeboard.com, Finaid.org, or Dinkytown.net. Each year, raise your contribution by the current college inflation rate (you'll find it at Collegeboard.com, under "Press," "News and Information," "College Costs"). That should keep you in the ballpark.

Or make it simpler. Decide on a rate of saving you can afford right now—say, $50 a week—and keep it up. Come college time, your resources will dictate what your kids can do (aided by their own ingenuity). A majority of students get a limited amount of free aid from the government and the schools themselves. Then they take loans. Two-thirds of undergraduates leave school with a median debt of $17,000 (half owe more, half owe less). The good news is that almost every student can afford to repay. A college education raises their prospects and their earning power.

AVERAGE COLLEGE COSTS, 2005–2006

	Tuition, fees	Room, board
Four-year private schools	$21,235	$7,791
Four-year public schools	5,491*	6,636
Two-year community colleges	2,191	N/A

* Surcharge for out-of-state students: $7,673.
SOURCE: College Board

HOW MUCH WILL YOU BE EXPECTED TO PAY?

There are two main sources of free college aid: government (federal and state) and the colleges themselves. Eligibility is based primarily on financial need—but "need" has nothing to do with what you think you can afford to pay. It's what the givers of aid say you ought to be able to afford.

Standard formulas determine how much you're expected to contribute toward your child's education. The government will want to know how much you earn, the size of your family, the amount of your savings and investments (not counting retirement savings, home equity, annuities, and life insurance cash values), and the net worth of any business you own. The private colleges have separate forms. In addition to what you told the government, they'll want to know the amount of your home equity, any unusual medical expenses, and how many other kids you have in school.

All these data go into a black box, where the Great Scholarship God riffles through your wallet. The formulas allocate certain percentages of your earnings and savings to your current and future expenses, including retirement accounts. The rest is considered available for higher education. You're given a dollar figure that you and your student have to pay, called the Expected Family Contribution. Your "financial need" is the difference between your expected contribution and the sticker price of the college your child wants to attend.

As an example, say that you're expected to pay $8,000 toward your child's freshman year. If you choose a $12,000 school, you're theoretically eligible for $4,000 in need-based financial aid. If you choose a $30,000 school, you're eligible for $22,000 in aid.

There's a hitch. Just because you're eligible for aid doesn't mean you'll get it. Maybe the college will fund your child in full. But maybe it will offer only part of the money, leaving you to worry about the rest. If you can't afford even the amount that the formula says you should contribute, that's your problem. From the school's point of view, you should have been saving more (which is exactly why you're reading this chapter). The definition of aid, by the way, includes government-subsidized student loans and campus jobs (work-study), as well as actual cash from scholarships, grants, and tuition discounts. So part of your aid package will have to be repaid.

How do you know in advance how much the Great Scholarship God will expect you to save? Two calculators will estimate your dreaded Expected Family Contribution—one at Collegeboard.com, the other (and more detailed) at Finaid.org. They don't come up with exactly the same amount, but they're in the ballpark. Use their findings as your savings target. Recalculate every few years, using your current income and assets, to see how close you are.

Many schools—mostly private but, increasingly, the more expensive publics—give extra money, called "merit aid," to particular students they want, even if they don't officially need the help. But you can't count on that. You *can* count on being financially pinched during the college years, but so will all your friends. It's a rite of passage. On your way home from your last child's graduation, you sigh, "Free at last."

ARE YOU DUMB TO SAVE?

Gossip says it's dumb to save because savers qualify for less college aid. That's often mathematically correct, but just because you qualify doesn't mean you'll get it. Furthermore, part of your aid comes in the form of loans, and people without any savings have to borrow more. What's the good of that? If your income suggests that you could have saved but didn't (you lived high, instead), you won't find the college-aid officers very sympathetic. They'll let you scramble, without turning a hair. There are better and worse ways to save for college, but those who save are always better off.

A 529 PLAN: THE COLLEGE SAVERS' GIFT

The simple, no-brainer way to save is through the tax-favored investment plans called 529s (named after the part of the tax code that authorizes them). The states set them up and each one is a little bit different. But they're a no-brainer *only* if you pick a plan that's low in cost. High-cost 529s chew into your savings, costing you more in fees than the value of the tax breaks you get. Many savers don't realize that, so I'm flashing it right up top. I love 529s, but only the sane and simple ones—noted below. Here's how they work:

You put money into the plan, in a lump sum or through regular, automatic deposits, and name a prospective student as beneficiary. There are two types of tax breaks:

1. Money that you earn on your plan investments—dividends, interest, and capital gains—pass tax-free if the beneficiary uses them to help pay for higher education (college, community college, trade school, even adult education).

2. In 25 states and the District of Columbia, you also get a tax deduction or tax credit on your state return for the contribution you make. Eight of these states * may even add a bit of matching money to a resident's account.

If the beneficiary decides not to go to college or to drop out, you can switch the money to another member of your family (including you, in case you ever want to return to school or take courses after you retire)†. If you withdraw any money for purposes other than education, you owe income taxes on the earnings plus a 10 percent penalty.

For detailed and comparative information on all the 529s, see Savingforcollege.com, or call the College Savings Plan Network (Collegesavings.org; 877-277-6496) to get material from specific states. Plans come in two varieties—a prepaid tuition plan that I'll call the "prepaid" and a pure savings-and-investment plan that I'll refer to simply as a 529. Here's what you need to know:

---

* Colorado, Louisiana, Pennsylvania, Maine, Michigan, Minnesota, Rhode Island, and Utah.

† Besides you, the "family" includes your children and stepchildren, grandchildren, siblings and stepsiblings, parents and grandparents (full or step), nieces and nephews, aunts and uncles, in-laws, family members' spouses (as long as they live with the family member), and first cousins.

Prepaid Plan

You'll find these in 25 states. They're super-simple, conservative, and designed for certainty. You put up money today to buy a fixed amount of tuition in the future. A few plans also cover room and board. Prices are based on current costs (often a little bit higher so that the fund can build a reserve). When your child finally goes to school, the portion you paid in advance will be covered in full, no matter how expensive college gets in the meantime. Buy eight semesters now and you'll get eight semesters in 2020, as easy as that. The states limit the number of years you can keep the plan. For example, you might have 10 years after the child reaches 18 to use up the value of the tuition credits or switch them to another member of the family.

Prepaid plans cover any public college or university in your state. If your child goes to a private college or a college out of state, the plan will provide a sum based on the cost of an in-state school (or your payment plus an interest rate).

Can you be sure the prepaids will pay when tuition time comes? Six states* guarantee their plans, so they're totally safe. The other plans can ask their state legislatures for additional funding if their finances fall short. I'm confident that you won't lose money in a prepaid. Even if a state changes or ends its plan (as several have), current investors will get full value for the money they've contributed so far.

One problem with prepaids: If you'll qualify for financial aid, they can sharply reduce the dollars you get from college work-study programs, federally subsidized student loans, and private college grants. But you're still fully eligible for federal grants and most state grants (pages 148–149), which may be enough. It's also

---

* Florida, Massachusetts, Mississippi, Ohio, Texas, Washington

possible that, by the time your child goes to school, the aid granters will have changed the rules.

Who should buy a prepaid plan? Buy if you want to feel that your child's future college is guaranteed, no matter what happens to your job or personal income. You're not looking for a growth investment with its scary ups and downs. You want certainty. You should also be reasonably sure that you'll continue to live in the state and that your child will attend a public college there.* Depending on the plan, either the owner or the beneficiary (or both) has to be a state resident.

If you buy, try to pay in lump sums (even serial lump sums) rather than sign up for an installment plan. Installments carry hidden interest rates in the 6 percent to 9 percent range, which might exceed the increase in future tuition costs.

Private-College Prepaid Plan

More than 240 private colleges and universities belong to this plan, called the Independent 529. Credits for future tuition payments are on sale at slightly discounted rates. You can use them at any participating school. For details and a list of the schools, go to Independent529.org or call 888-718-7878. You get no state tax deductions for contributions to this private plan. But all your investment gains still pass tax free.

529 Plan for Savings and Investments

Here, you get no guarantees. Instead, you put your money into one or more of the plan's investment pools (mostly mutual funds). Over time, their value grows (you hope). You use the proceeds, tax-free,

---

* An exception is Alabama, which takes out-of-staters.

for any of the direct expenses of higher education—tuition, fees, books, room and board, computers, and other equipment. All accredited schools in the U.S. are eligible as well as schools in some countries abroad, so you're not forced to stay in-state. You can join another state's 529 if you don't like your own. There's no limit to the amount of time the money can stay in the plan so long as there's a named beneficiary who's a family member. Most states put no age limits on the beneficiary, either. If your child drops out of school, you can leave the money in his or her name in hopes of a change of heart. Or switch the account to someone else. Or switch it to your name, during your midlife crisis, and use it to train for a new career. Or fund an education for all of your grandchildren. Even a newborn is a legal beneficiary.

These 529s aren't as cut-and-dried as the prepaid plans. You have a few choices to make, but they aren't complicated.

- *Which state's plan do you use?* Look first at your own state's 529. It could be the best if its fees are low (see below), and especially if it offers extra tax breaks. Some states let you deduct a portion of your investment on your state tax return. Some even make a cash contribution to your account. If the plan is expensive, however, and you get no state tax breaks, jump to a state with low fees and solid investment choices.
- *How should you purchase the plan?* You can buy directly from the state (these are called "direct-sold plans") or buy through a stockbroker or planner ("adviser-sold plans"). Both types are listed on the state websites. But only one choice makes financial sense: Buy from the state! It's free! You just fill in a form, pick your investments (see page 141), and mail a check. To find your state's plan, go to Savingforcollege.com or Collegesavings.org.

Savers who choose an adviser-sold plan will have to pay a sales commission. The mutual funds you get will charge high annual fees. Counting all costs, your expenses will probably exceed your tax savings. If you're going to use a broker anyway, a mutual fund inside a 529 is a better deal than the same fund outside the plan, as long as you're not also paying a high state administrative fee. Still, it's a crummy way to buy.

- *What are the fees?* It's often hard to figure them out because state disclosure are often so poor. Here's what to look for in the plan description that the state will send you:

  1. The fees charged by the state for running the program, expressed as a percentage of the value of your account. Look for a plan that costs 0.3 percent a year or less. Fees of 0.5 percent and up are just too high.

  2. The fees charged by the managers who run the mutual funds in your 529. The lowest-cost funds come from Vanguard and they're only in direct-sold plans. You might pay as little as 0.025 percent a year. By contrast, adviser-sold funds could cost 1 percent or more. That's a huge difference, compounded over time.

  3. Flat-dollar fees, charged by some states, for enrollment or to maintain your account. These fees take the largest bite out of small investments. States might waive them for residents, large accounts, accounts receiving automatic contributions, or accounts invested in fixed-income funds.

  4. Bundled fees. A few states quote you a single price, which covers both their own fees and the fees for money management. These tend to be plans with lower costs—typically, less than 0.7 percent a year. The list, at this writing: California, Iowa, Michigan, Minnesota, Missouri, and New York. Oregon doesn't bundle its fees but it's low-cost, too. Lousiana's excellent plan is open only to its own residents, alas.

- *Which states give savers the very best deal and are open to everyone?* At this writing, I have three favorites. The cost quotes, below, combine each state's program fees with the management fees for the plan's lowest-cost funds:

Ohio's College Advantage 529 Savings Plan, for as little as 0.35 percent per year. (Collegeadvantage.com; 800-233-6734.)

Utah's Educational Savings Plan Trust, for as little as 0.275 percent, plus $5 for each $1,000 invested up to an annual maximum of $25. (Uesp.org; 800-418-2551.)

Virginia's Education Savings Trust, for as little as 0.258 percent, plus one $25 fee. (Virginia529.com; 888-567-0540.)

- *How can you compare the costs of other plans?* Use the 529 College Savings Expense Analyzer, developed by the National Association of Securities Dealers at Nasd.com (look under "Tools Calculators Games"). It will show you, in dollars, how much money you leave on the table when you pay high fees.

- *Should you buy through payroll deduction?* At a growing number of companies, you can ask that money be taken from your paycheck and invested automatically in a 529. I love payroll deductions but not necessarily this one. The plan the company chooses might not be based in your state, so you'll lose any state tax deduction available. If it is in your state, it's probably a broker-sold plan with high commissions. Compare the company's offer with what you can get by going directly to the state. If the direct-sold plan is cheaper, or you prefer the 529 in another state, set up your automated payments through your bank rather than through payroll deduction.

- *Should you change the plan you have?* Sure. Why not? If you've just discovered that you accidentally bought an expensive plan, and if your state tax benefits don't save it, there's no reason to stay. Roll your money into a different 529. The new plan will tell you how to proceed. There are usually no penalties for switching, but some states charge small fees. A few states, including New York and Pennsylvania, tax the earnings on 529s if they're moved to an out-of-state plan. They may even bill you for tax deductions you took in the past.

HOW YOU CAN PAY MORE FOR A 529
THAN THE TAXES YOU SAVE

Assume that you have $5,000 in your 529 account, invested in bonds and earning interest at 5 percent. You make $250 for the year and save $62.50 in tax in the 25 percent bracket.

In a high-cost plan, your annual fees might come to 1.5 percent in state program fees and money management costs. You pay $75. Your expenses exceed your tax savings by $12.50. Put another way, you're giving $12.50 to middlemen rather than keeping it for college tuition.

In a low-cost plan, you might pay just 0.3 percent. That's a mere $15 for the year. Your tax savings earn $47.50 more than you owe in costs. You have that much extra money invested for your child's future.

The comparisons look even worse if the $250 you earned came from a capital gain, taxable at 15 percent. Your tax-sheltered 529 has now saved you just $37.50 in tax. In the high-cost plan, you're paying double that amount in fees. The low-cost plan, however, still brings you out ahead.

- *How should you invest the money you're putting into a 529?* The plans offer several options, including an all-stock fund, a fixed-income fund, a mixed stock-and-bond fund, and several age-related choices.

    For a smart, one-step, sleep-tight decision, choose an age-related fund. Its investments change, depending on how old your child is. When the child is young, the fund will lean heavily toward stocks for growth. As your child grows older, it will lean toward safer, fixed-income investments, so you're sure to have cash when college expenses start. Some age-related programs have gotten pretty fancy, letting you choose among three or more investment portfolios: aggressive, moderate, or conservative. The aggressive fund will stay substantially in stocks, even when your child approaches freshman year. That's okay for high-income people; if their stocks tank, they can write the tuition check from other accounts they have. But aggressive strategies are risky for people who'll definitely need their 529 plan to pay the bills. What will you do if the market drops and doesn't recover over the next four years? For true security, choose an age-based fund that will be mostly in cash when your child turns 18.

If you don't want an age-related fund, you'll have to manage your own 529 account. Most plans let you transfer money from one mutual fund to another, once a year. You'll have to keep monitoring this. When your child is 16, you'll want different investments than those you chose when the child was 8 (see pages 151–153). But why bother with all this cogitating? In an age-related fund, you get timely, personal money management automatically. That's exactly the kind of help busy people need.

- *When should you start saving?* It's never too soon, but might be too late. In a few states, your money may have to stay in the plan for two to four years before it can be withdrawn. In most states, however, you can start a 529 when your child is 17, grab the state tax deduction, and immediately take out the money for tuition. Not bad.

- *Who can contribute to the plan?* Any warm body—relatives, friends, your children themselves, Santa Claus. Most states let them contribute to the plan directly. In some, they have to give the parents the money and let the parents deposit it.

- *How much can you contribute?* As much as you want, up to $200,000 or $300,000 per child, depending on the state. Not that you plan to save that much by next Tuesday morning. My point is that 529s aren't limited, as so many other tax-favored savings plans are. With investment gains, your account could grow even larger—enough for a lifetime of degrees.

There's a special tax angle here for wealthy contributors. You get a break on the federal gift tax when the money goes into a 529. In 2006, you can give up to $12,000 a year to any recipient, gift-tax free. If you're giving to a 529, however, you can make up to five years' worth of gifts in advance. That's $60,000 for an individual or $120,000 for a couple, all at once (after that, you can't give the recipient any tax-free money until five years have passed). If you die, that money won't be counted in your estate. Surprisingly, the gift doesn't have to be permanent. You can take it back, on payment of taxes and the 10 percent penalty on any earnings. (Send this info to grandma, if she has bucks to spare!)

- *Who owns the 529?* Parents should. Register it in your name. You can then decide what to invest in, how much money to distribute, and who the beneficiary will be. You're also apt to get more college aid if the 529 is owned by the parent rather than a grandparent or the child.
- *Do 529 plans limit your eligibility for college aid?* No more than most other savings plans, and less than some. When the government and private colleges calculate how much they think you can pay, they count just 5.6 percent of the money in a parent-owned 529. The rest effectively "isn't there" for the purpose of awarding aid. In real life, you'll probably spend more of the money than that. But 529 funds used to pay for school will not be counted as part of your income when you apply for aid next year. You can't do any better than that.

If your student owns the 529, the aid award could decline a lot. Up to 35 percent of the student's assets are considered available to pay for school. If a grandparent owns the 529, it's not counted as a family asset. But any payment the grandparent makes is normally treated as student income and will reduce the amount of next year's aid. For families with modest incomes ($50,000 or less), the 529 doesn't count at all.

- *What if your student gets scholarships and doesn't need the 529?* You can remove an amount equal to the scholarships from the 529, paying taxes on the earnings but no penalty. (And, of course, you can always keep the account, naming a new beneficiary.)

- *What if you move?* You can transfer your 529 money to another state's plan or leave it alone and open a second plan in your new state. A few states tax the money your investments earn in out-of-state plans. They might also tax any earnings you transfer from your old plan into a new one—check it out, before you switch. In any state, however, your earnings are free of federal tax.

- *What's a good printed source for detailed information on 529s?* I recommend *The Best Way to Save for College: A Complete Guide to 529 Plans,* by Joseph F. Hurley ($22.95).

- *Can you spend your way to college savings?* Two programs—Babymint.com and Upromise.com—link with credit cards that offer cash rebates. You earn up to 1 percent of the charges you put on the card (with a few merchants offering more). These rebates go into a cash account, from which they can be swept into a 529. At this writing, Upromise works with 529 plans in five states. Babymint works with all of them, as long as they take third-party contributions. These rebates aren't big, in dollar terms. They're not worth opening a separate 529 to get. But if the plan works with the 529 you have, why not?

MORE THAN YOU WANT TO KNOW
ABOUT 529S AND TAXES*

The government hands out tax breaks like cupcakes to people paying for higher education. Tax-exempt savings in 529s are only the
start. You also get tax deductions or credits on your annual tax return, for the tuition and fees you pay. But you can't collect one tax
break on top of another. There's only one cupcake per customer.

A nice, simple principle, right? You can use your prepaid plan or
529 only to cover college expenses that haven't been used already
to claim another tax deduction or credit. This is Taxland, of course.
What's simple to say isn't simple to figure out.

There are two different tax breaks you might claim on your tax
return. Each of them "uses up" a different amount of college tuition.
Your 529 savings can be spent only on expenses that haven't already
been "used." Here's a summary of how these tax breaks work:

1. *The Hope tax credit.* Good for the first two years your child is in
   school at least half-time. If you meet the income test †, you can
   lower your taxes by 100 percent of the first $1,100 you spend on
   the child's tuition and 50 percent of the second $1,100. That
   "uses up" $2,200 in college expenses. Anyone who takes the
   Hope credit on his or her tax return can spend money from a
   529 to cover all education expenses higher than $2,200.
2. *The Lifetime Learning tax credit.* Good for any school year, and
   even for single courses. As long as you meet the same income
   test that's used for the Hope, you can deduct 20 percent of as

---

* Don't bother reading this if your kids are still young! It's only for parents dealing with
this issue now.
† In 2006, the full credit goes to singles and heads of household with adjusted gross incomes up to $45,000, phasing out at $55,000; and couples up to $90,000, phasing out at
$110,000. These limits rise with the inflation rate.

much as $10,000 spent on tuition expenses (that's for everyone in your family who's studying that year). The credit itself comes to a maximum of $2,000 but it "uses up" $10,000 in tuition. If you take the maximum Lifetime Learning credit, you can use 529 savings only for education expenses higher than $10,000.

For details on the tax rules, go to Irs.gov and search for the government's explanatory guide, "Publication 970: Tax Benefits for Education."* The rules for using tax-free money from Coverdell Education Savings Accounts and qualified U.S. Savings Bonds (both discussed below) are the same as those for 529s. Whew.

OTHER COLLEGE SAVINGS PLANS

Many parents save for college in plain-vanilla mutual funds or brokerage accounts. They give you total flexibility but cost you important tax breaks that will put more money into your child's education account.

Of the other tax-favored college savings plans, none are as good as a low-cost—emphasize *low-cost*—529. If you have any of these competing plans already, you can switch the money into a 529. Here are your options and why I generally rate them second-best. (Okay, they're still best for some uses, which I note.)

Coverdell Education Savings Account (ESA). It works like a 529. You invest your money in mutual funds and the earnings grow tax-free if they're used for education. But you can contribute only $2,000 a year for each child up to his or her eighteenth birthday (longer, if the child has "special needs"). You get no state tax break

---

* A deduction for tuition expenses expired in 2006. It's possible that Congress will renew it. If that happens, you'll have one more tax break to consider. The expired provision lets you deduct either $2,000 or $4,000 in tuition expenses, depending on your income. Any 529 money could be used only for expenses higher than that.

on the money you put in and you face income limitations.* Any balance left in a Coverdell has to be used before the beneficiary reaches 30 (although you can name a new beneficiary). There's a 10 percent penalty on earnings spent on anything other than education. If you started with a Coverdell and now want a 529, you can remove Coverdell money tax-free in any year that you make an equal or greater contribution to a prepaid plan or 529 for the same beneficiary.

The plus: You can use ESAs for the expenses of private school, kindergarten through twelfth grade, or equipment needed for public school, such as a laptop computer. A 529, by contrast, is good only for higher education.

U.S. Savings Bonds. This tax break applies to people 24 and up who have bought Series EE bonds issued since January 1990, or any Series I Bond. You can use the proceeds, tax-free, toward the cost of higher education for yourself, your spouse, or a dependent. The only requirement is that your income fall within certain limits † in the year you want to redeem the bonds and pay tuition. If you think that your income will exceed these limits, you have an out: You can cash in the bonds tax-free if you contribute an equal amount to a prepaid tuition plan, a 529 savings plan, or a Coverdell ESA for yourself, your spouse, or a dependent.

The plus: If you don't use the bonds for higher education, you still get the earnings free of state and local tax. For more information, see Savingsbonds.gov.

An Individual Retirement Account. Normally, you owe income taxes plus a 10 percent penalty on withdrawals from a traditional IRA prior to age 59½. The penalty is waived, however, if you use

---

* To set up an ESA, your adjusted gross income must be less than $110,000 for singles and $220,000 for married couples filing jointly.

† In 2006, the tax breaks are phased out for single people with adjusted gross incomes between $63,100 and $78,100 and couples between $94,700 and $124,700. These limits rise with the inflation rate.

the money to pay for higher education. If you have a Roth IRA, you can withdraw your own contribution tax-free at any time. You'll owe taxes on any Roth earnings withdrawn before 59½ but, again, the penalty is waived.

The plus: You can use IRA money for anything, not just education.

WATCHING FOR SUNSET

Under current law, some of the tax breaks available for 529s will vanish—or "sunset"—in 2010. Instead of being tax-free, distributions may be taxed in the child's bracket. Contributions to Coverdell ESAs could drop to just $500 a year. Will that happen? Who knows? I'm betting that Congress will continue its special favors to college savers. If not, you can still do okay with 529s, provided that your plan's costs are low.

WHEN THE TIME COMES: FINDING STUDENT AID

This isn't a handbook on finding and applying for student aid. But I can tell you where to get help.

For federal government aid, both grants and loans: Go to Studentaid.ed.gov for tons of information about federal programs and the application process. Fafsa.ed.gov includes the critical FAFSA, or Free Application for Federal Student Aid. When you fill in that form, you get a Student Aid Report, showing your expected family contribution. All colleges, public and private, will want to see it. They'll construct an aid package based in part on what the government says.

For private college aid, go to Collegeboard.com. Look for the CSS/Financial Aid PROFILE, a supplemental financial aid application. It's used by about 600 colleges, universities, and scholarship funds for awarding student aid from private sources. You fill it out just once, online, and direct it to any participating school. This site includes information on government programs, too. A huge databank lets you research schools, sorting them by type and cost. For private colleges and universities that don't participate in PROFILE, you'll have to fill in individual financial aid forms. Check the deadlines, to be sure your application arrives on time.

For state grants and loans, search for your state's student aid website online. High school guidance offices should have the information, too (assuming your school can still afford the "luxury" of guidance for higher education, in this world of tax and budget cuts).

For general information, try Finaid.org and the National Association of Student Financial Aid Administrators at Nasfaa.org.

OTHER WAYS TO PAY

Federally subsidized Stafford student loans. Your student can borrow limited amounts.* While they're in school, high-income students have to pay interest; the Stafford is free for everyone else. When students leave school, repayments start—always at a low, variable interest rate. A good idea? You bet. It's the student's education. When the family isn't wealthy, he or she should pay. Stafford student loans can be had directly from the federal government, through special programs set up by participating schools. Alternatively, they're offered through private banks and credit unions and specialized student lenders such as Sallie Mae (Salliemae.com). For additional information, see Studentaid.ed.gov or Collegeboard.com. These sites tell you about the federal PLUS loans for parents, too.

---

*Freshmen, $2,625; sophomores, $3,500; juniors and seniors, $5,500; graduate students, $8,500.

Federal PLUS loans for parents. Around 10 percent of parents with students in school borrow money through PLUS. Rates are low compared with those on other loans. A good idea? I hate to see parents borrow large sums of money when they're getting close to retirement age. But if you must, compare the rate on PLUS loans with the after-tax cost of borrowing against home equity.

Private loan programs. If Stafford loans aren't enough, students can borrow from banks at reasonable rates. Special student loan programs defer principal and interest payments until the student leaves school. For parents, the school may offer a monthly payment plan. A good idea? Only if you and your child aren't taking on too much debt. Maybe you should consider a cheaper school.

A home-equity loan. Interest is tax-deductible on loans up to $100,000. A good idea? Maybe, if interest rates are low, you have plenty of home equity, and could still pay your bills (including the loan repayments) if you had to retire earlier than you expected.

Stocks or mutual funds that have gained in value. Give them away to your child and let the child sell. Assuming that he or she is in the low, 15 percent tax bracket, the gains will be taxed at only 5 percent. You can give up to $12,000 a year tax-free ($24,000, if your spouse gives, too). A good idea? Sure, if you planned it this way and if you aren't expecting need-based financial aid—too much money in a student's name will wipe out the possibility of an award. Just be sure you can afford it before you give those stocks away.

Grandparents. Borrow only if it won't weaken their retirement security.

DOES IT PAY TO SAVE MONEY IN A CHILD'S NAME?

Yes and no.

No, if you hope to qualify for college aid. When computing how much a family ought to pay, both the government and the colleges treat children's savings different from parents' savings. They expect students to use up to 35 percent of their savings for college every year. But they expect parents to use no more than 5.6 percent of their eligible assets. By keeping all the savings in a parent's name, you look "poorer" in the aid formula, and eligible for more help.

But *yes*, the child should hold the money if aid isn't an issue (and if you're sure that he or she won't spend it). At this writing, a child can collect up to $1,700 in unearned income (interest, dividends, royalties) and pay no tax. Higher amounts are taxed in your bracket, if the child is under 14. At 14 and older, however, the earnings are taxed in the child's bracket, which is probably lower than yours.

What if you've already put some money into a child's name and wish you hadn't? Savings owned by a minor under the Uniform Transfers to Minors Act (or Uniform Gifts to Minors Act) can be switched into a 529. Ask your plan how.

A STRATEGY FOR COLLEGE INVESTING

Personally, I'd choose either a prepaid plan or an age-related fund in a 529. But if you want to go it alone, here's a useful investment strategy. It's still age-related, but you decide what to invest in and when to sell one fund and buy another. No tax breaks, however. When you sell an investment at a profit, you have to report the capital gain.

For children up to age 12. Save money regularly. The sooner you start, the less college will effectively cost because you'll be paying part of the bill with money that your money earns. To appreciate the value of early savings, take a look at the table on page 16. Put your savings into a mix of U.S. and international stock–owning index mutual funds (Chapter 7). Don't try to buy and sell as market conditions change. Too often, you'll guess wrong. Just faithfully put your money away, month after month, in good times and bad, and reinvest the dividends.

For children 12 to 14. Deposit new savings into bond mutual funds (Chapter 7). At the same time, start moving some of the money you previously saved out of stocks and into bonds. Exactly when you move the money will depend on market conditions (sell high, not low—duh—but that's not always as easy as you think). By the time your child reaches 14, about 25 percent of your college money should be in bonds or other fixed-interest investments. They may lose some purchasing power, after taxes and college inflation. But that's a small worry compared with the risk that stock prices will drop and not recover by the time the college bills come due. You're moving toward guaranteeing your child's freshman year.

For children 15 and up. Gradually move the rest of your money out of stock funds and into safe investments. Start selling the bond funds and putting the proceeds into bank certificates of deposit or money-market mutual funds. By the time your child matriculates, your entire college fund should no longer be at risk. Additional investments made in these years should also go into safety-first instruments, not into stocks or bonds.

Some financial advisers want you to stay substantially in stocks, even when your child enters school. They're gambling that, by your child's junior and senior year, stocks will be up and you'll have extra money to pay. Fine, I love it . . . but what if stocks fall? It hardly matters, if you could pay for college anyway. But sticking with stocks makes no sense if, in a bad market, you'd have to borrow (or borrow even more) to get your child through school.

If you don't start saving until your child is 13 or 14. Buying stocks now is a major risk. Consider bond mutual funds instead.

If you didn't save or had your children late. You may not be able to save for college and retirement at the same time. In this pickle, save for retirement first. Your children can borrow their way through school but you won't be able to borrow your way through your old age.

For a more extended discussion of college investing, go to "Saving for College," a Vanguard PlainTalk guide at Vanguard.com.

DON'T GET SCAMMED

One happy day, you might get a happy letter about student aid. Your high school student has been "specially selected" to attend a college scholarship seminar! He or she qualifies for large amounts of free money! Scholarship experts are coming to town, who will "guarantee" to get you more aid than you could yourself! They even know secret ways of getting your child into a dream school! Just sign here for a year of personal service at $1,500 or more.

It's all baloney. Here's what you'll get for your money: Standard information on how to fill in the FAFSA federal aid form. A brochure about how to write a good college application essay. Lists of "private scholarships" you might apply for. Impractical ideas, such as using all your cash savings to prepay your mortgage so the savings won't show on your student aid form. (If you do that, where do you get the cash to pay the college bills? You'll have to borrow it back on a home-equity loan and pay interest.) You get the idea. They fill your head with stuff that sounds good but really isn't. Besides, you can find the same information free at the websites I've mentioned in this chapter, including lists of private scholarships. There are *no* secrets to getting college aid. Don't be scammed into paying.

WHAT IF YOU'RE STILL REPAYING YOUR OWN STUDENT LOANS?

If you have young kids and you're still paying off your own student loans, get rid of that debt as fast as you can. Put yourself on a quick-repayment plan. Once the loans have cleared, you can redirect those payments into college savings for your children's school. Don't consolidate the loans, stretching them out over a longer term. That lowers your monthly payments but raises the total interest cost, making it harder to save for other things. Consolidation would be better than default, which shows on your credit history and can put you in debt-collection hell. But squeezing to pay is better than both.

AUTOMATE IT

This book is all about cutting through the nonsense that makes life's money decisions seem complex. They're actually easy, once you know the right principles and good products, and saving for college is no exception. First, remember your order of business, the "life's list" that this book is built on: Save for retirement, eliminate consumer debt, and build a Cushion Fund, all through automated payments. With these three essentials on track, people with children should consider a 529. Buy directly from your state, if you get a tax advantage, or from Ohio, Utah, or Virginia if you don't. Never buy through a salesperson—it costs you more than the taxes you save. Automate your college savings, too. That's the surest (and easiest) way of building the fund you want.

7. BETTER INVESTING

Good News: The Smartest Investments Are the Simplest Ones

Everyone needs good, long-term financial investments but never before has finding them seemed so hard. There's so much to choose from, you hardly know where to start. Should you buy stocks? The list runs to thousands, and some of them turn out to be frauds. How about mutual funds? Every ad screams "I'm the best." An army of salespeople stands ready to help—all peddling investments loaded with fees and producing subpar returns. Even in company retirement plans, you have to sort through a dozen or more funds, with little or no help. What's a hopeful investor to do?

Ignore it all! You don't need 99.9 percent of what Wall Street is selling. It's expensive, unsuitable, or stupid. Most investments are designed to profit the brokers, banks, and insurance companies, not you. They should carry a warning label—"Beware! This financial product may be injurious to your wealth!"

Happily, a few sensible options have emerged from this vast financial wasteland. They're simple investments that everyone can use, with dependable long-term results. "Simple" doesn't mean "simpleminded." Under the surface, these products are super-sophisticated and complex. They copy the strategies used by big-time professional investors who manage billions of dollars for pension funds and college endowments. Yet they're easy to handle yourself.

Don't let the word "easy" put you off, either. These aren't mere stopgap investments, usable only until you have the time to find something better. They *are* better—offering lower risk and superior long-term returns. Plus, they fit perfectly into the lives of busy people who don't want to worry about their money every minute.

Among these investments, the best are low-cost. *Cost is the single best predictor of future returns!* The less you pay, the faster your money is likely to grow.

INVESTING 101

Before we go further, you'll need to learn a few investment terms. Not many, I promise. Most of Wall Street's jargon relates to financial products that you wouldn't want anyway. The smart and sensible choices can be fully explained using just the words that are listed here:

I'll start with *stocks* (or *shares*), the investment you hear about the most. They represent a tiny bit of ownership in a corporation. If you own 100 shares of Microsoft, for example, you own 100 bits of its profits, its dividends, and its underlying value. When a company grows and prospers, the market price of its stock goes up. If the company staggers or loses popularity, the price of its stock goes down. You don't know how well any particular company's stock will perform, over the long term. But stocks—on average— build more wealth than other investments do (much better than real estate, you may be surprised to learn). For this reason, long-term investors put the majority of their money there.

The general word for ownership interest is *equity*. You might say, "I've invested in equities," meaning you bought stocks, or "I chose an equity mutual fund," one that invests in stocks. (Similarly, *home equity* means your ownership interest in your house.)

A *dividend* is a small piece of the profits that some companies pay out to investors, usually quarterly or twice a year.

A *bond* represents debt. It's an IOU. When you "buy" a bond, you are lending money to the entity that issued it—a government body or corporation. You earn interest on the money you've lent, which is normally paid to you twice a year.

Bonds are scheduled to last for a fixed period of time. At the end of the period, they're said to *mature*. At that point, you get your money back. Sometimes, the issuer repays the bond before maturity; that's known as a *call*.

Bond prices are steadier than the prices of stocks. You own them to limit your risk. *Treasury bonds* are issued by the federal government. *Municipal bonds* are issued by cities, states, and various public authorities (they're known as *munis* and their interest is tax-free). *Corporate bonds* are issued by corporations such as General Electric or Intel. Mutual funds that invest primarily in bonds are called bond funds or *fixed-income* funds.

When you invest the easy way, you'll be buying shares in a *mutual fund*. A mutual fund is a big pool of money, contributed by thousands of people just like you. The manager of that money invests it in stocks, bonds, or both. Your share in the fund gives you a tiny ownership interest in all the fund's investments, so you are spreading your money around. That's a sensible thing to do.

As a mutual-fund shareholder, you receive a piece of the dividends that the fund's investments earn. You can use those dividends to buy more shares automatically (called *dividend reinvestment*)— an easy way to grow your wealth. There are many, many different types of mutual funds—technology funds, gold funds, health-care funds, utility funds, and on and on. You don't need any of them. The best funds own all of these stocks at once. I'll be telling you more about them.

A *security* is a general word for a "paper" investment, such as stocks or bonds (it doesn't include "hard" investments such as gold coins or real estate). In the old days, it was a real piece of paper showing that you owned a particular stock or bond. Nowadays, a security (including a share in a mutual fund) is generally a computer blip with your name attached. Your proof of ownership is a mailed or electronic acknowledgment. If you deal with a stockbroker, you will get a mailed or online *confirmation* when you make a purchase or sale.

An *asset* is anything you own that has monetary value. Your stocks, bonds, mutual funds, retirement accounts, and bank accounts are all assets. So are your home, cars, and any real-estate investments, along with good jewelry and antiques.

Asset allocation refers to the way you've split your money among various types of investments—say, 60 percent in stocks, 35 percent in bonds, and 5 percent in cash. You'll read a lot about this strategy later.

Diversification means spreading your money over many different kinds of investments. This reduces your risk. When the market value of one type of investment is going down, another will probably be going up, so your total portfolio doesn't take as big a loss. The right mutual fund diversifies your money automatically.

Your *portfolio* refers to all the investments you own. It's a simple, descriptive word that means "everything." You probably didn't even know you had a portfolio, but you do.

The *market* refers to the activity of buying and selling. In a *bull market*, prices rise. In a *bear market*, they go down. How do you remember which is which? In bear markets, you say "Grrrr."

When you sell one stock or bond and buy another, you make a *trade*. The buyer thinks the price of the stock is going up. The seller thinks it isn't. The function of a market is to bring buyers and sellers together at a price they both think is fair at the time.

A retirement plan, such as a 401(k) or Individual Retirement

Account (IRA) is *tax-deferred*. Your investment gains aren't taxed until you take the money out. *Taxable accounts* are investments outside a retirement plan. You owe income taxes every year on the interest and dividends these investments earn. If you sell a taxable investment at a profit, you'll owe a *capital gains tax*.

The *economy* refers to general business conditions—interest rates, inflation, profits, unemployment, wages, imports and exports, all the real-life things that affect our spending and our standard of living.

That's it. A "bluffer's guide" to the securities markets. Drop these words into any investment conversation and you'll make it through!

NO WORRY INVESTING: THE SHORT LIST

I'm partial to the "pay-no-attention" way of financial life. Investing is something you shouldn't have to worry about. You want a plan that runs by itself and can give you reliable long-term results with no heart-stopping accidents along the way. Three types of mutual funds fill the bill—target retirement funds, lifecycle funds, and index funds.

Target Retirement Mutual Funds: Choose Once and Forget It

These are my favorite sleep-tight funds, the easiest investments in the universe. They're new and, where offered, already hugely popular. People who hear about them feel that little click in the mind that says, "Yes, this is going to work."

With a target retirement fund, you have to decide only one thing: when you think you might retire. Pick a fund designed for approximately that retirement date, put your money there, and forget about it. There are funds for retirement in 2010, 2015, 2020,

2025, 2030, 2035, 2040, and 2045, depending on the fund company you choose—and more years will be added as time goes on. Each fund owns a mix of stocks and bonds that is suitable for a person retiring in that decade. For example:

- *If you're in your twenties, thirties, or forties.* Retirement is far away. You'd pick a fund aimed at a year between 2030 and 2045. Funds invested for that many years own mostly stocks for long-term growth. They also own a small percentage of bonds, to limit your risk. If you were picking your own, separate investments, this is just what you'd want.
- *If you're in your fifties and sixties.* Retirement is in view. You'd pick a fund aimed at the years between 2010 and 2025. They're still invested in stocks, but keep a higher percentage of their money in bonds. The closer you get to your probable retirement date, the more conservative your fund becomes.

Target retirement funds run on automatic pilot. They gradually change their mix of investments as the years go by. Today, a 2025 fund is heavily into stocks. Ten years from now—when you're that much closer to retirement—your fund will own a somewhat smaller percentage of stocks and a slightly higher percentage of bonds. You never have to rejigger your own investments as you age. The fund does that for you, all the time.

Your fund doesn't come to an end when the target date is reached. You can keep it for as many more years as you like. If you don't retire, you're still okay. Thanks to the way the fund invests, your money is positioned to give you the option of retiring, if that's what you want.

As you grow even older, target retirement funds become straight income funds, invested for dividends and interest while protecting your principal from risk. So they're still no-worry mutual funds, with money managed in a suitable way.

Some company 401(k) plans offer target retirement funds. They're pretty new but spreading fast.

For investments outside a 401(k), including an Individual Retirement Account, you can choose among several mutual-fund companies. Here are three:

1. *The Vanguard Group*, with six funds called "Target Retirement" funds. These are the lowest-cost funds, by far. At this writing, they charge around 0.22 percent a year. Low-cost funds give you better returns than similar high-cost funds because they leave more of your money in your account to grow. In any year, Vanguard tends to allocate less of your money to stocks than the competition does. But thanks to the magic of low fees, these conservative funds can give you the same net returns that more aggressive funds do. The more you contribute or the better the market performs, the faster your dollars build in a low-cost fund. (Vanguard.com; 877-662-7447. There's a $10 annual fee on small accounts.)

2. *Fidelity Investments*, with ten "Freedom Funds," costing 0.69 percent to 0.79 percent, depending on the target year. You might think it's no big deal to pay Fidelity an extra 0.5 percent a year, but the dollars mount up. If you invested $400 a month for 30 years in both Vanguard and Fidelity, and the funds grew 8 percent a year, the Fidelity fund would cost you $52,748 more than Vanguard did. Fidelity holds a higher percentage of its money in stocks. It's betting on higher investment returns, to cover its costs and give something more to investors, too. (Fidelity.com; 800-343-3548)

3. *T. Rowe Price*, with nine "Retirement Funds," costing from 0.78 percent to 0.81 percent. T. Rowe Price invests the most aggressively of this group. At retirement, you'd still be 60 percent in stocks, compared with about 35 percent at Vanguard and 45 percent at Fidelity (you can check the latest comparisons at

their websites). Aggressive investments can potentially deliver more growth, over the long run. If that occurs, you'll retire with a higher nest egg, after costs. But funds like these rise and fall more in price than other funds do. You have to be prepared to stay the course in a year when the market drops. (Troweprice.com; 800-638-5660)

Other mutual-fund groups offer target retirement investments, too, mostly at a higher cost. Always compare costs before you buy.

Of the three groups I've mentioned, I'd personally opt for Vanguard for its lower cost. If you're investing outside a retirement plan, where your annual gains are taxable, Vanguard offers a second advantage: It invests through a type of fund called an *index fund*. Indexing reduces the annual tax you'll owe on investment gains, leaving you with higher returns after tax. For a full explanation, see page 165.

But that's just my choice. You might prefer the high stock allocation at T. Rowe Price, in hopes of getting more long-term growth. Either way, you're going to be fine. Any of these funds is an excellent choice compared with the (probably) unplanned mix of stocks and funds you might own now. Your current investments may not be diversified enough, and carry more long-term risk than you realize.

Here is the most important thing to know about choosing a target retirement fund: To achieve its purpose it should be the *only* fund you own. At the very least you should keep most of your money there. A target retirement fund plots your investments carefully. For any age, the manager keeps an appropriate balance between the percentage of money you hold in stocks and the percentage you keep in bonds. If you own many other mutual funds, that careful plan goes down the drain. You'll wind up with too much or too little in stocks, depending on the market and on the funds you've picked. By concentrating your investments in a single target fund, your retirement money will always be arranged in an intelligent way.

"But wait a minute," you say, "I thought I was supposed to diversify. With just one fund, don't I have all my eggs in one basket?" Yes and no. It's one basket because you own a single fund. But your fund contains all the different kinds of assets that you ought to own—large and small U.S. stocks, real-estate stocks, international stocks, and U.S. government and corporate bonds. With just one, simple investment choice, you get it all.

I love target retirement funds—they do everything you need. They diversify your money. Choose appropriate assets for your age and situation. Hold down your costs. Save you from irretrievable mistakes. Limit your risk by keeping the proper balance between stocks and bonds when market prices change. If you hired an investment adviser to do these things for you, you'd pay 1 percent to 2 percent a year, plus the cost of the investments that the manager chose. A target retirement fund comes with built-in investment advice, and at a fraction of the price.

Lifecycle Mutual Funds: Simple, With More Choice

If you're investing primarily through a 401(k) or 403(b), you might be offered a different—but almost as easy—choice, called a lifecycle fund. It's in the federal Thrift Savings Plan, too. Like a target retirement fund, a lifecycle fund is fully diversified. This single investment gives you all the types of stocks and bonds you ought to own, in a single package.

Lifecycle funds differ from target retirement funds in one big way. You get to choose the specific mix of stocks and bonds you want. A "growth" fund will hold around 75 percent of its money in stocks and 25 percent in bonds. A "moderate" fund leans toward 60 percent in stocks and 40 percent in bonds. A "conservative" fund might drop to 25 percent stocks and 75 percent bonds and cash. There are other flavors, too.

Lifecycle funds do not change their investments over time. A growth portfolio that's 75 percent in stocks will stay that way, give or take a few percentage points. When you're young, the growth investment is exactly the right choice. But when you hit 50, you might want to switch to a moderate mix. "Switching" means that you sell your first fund and buy a different one. You can do that tax-free in a retirement account, such as a 401(k) or Individual Retirement Account. But if you're investing outside a retirement account, selling your first fund will trigger a tax on the profit you made. That's something to think about in advance. You should choose a portfolio that you're pretty sure you can live with for a very long time.

As you can see, a lifecycle fund requires one or two more decisions than a target retirement fund does. In general, you should choose your investment mix by age. Be aggressive in your twenties, thirties, and forties, moderate in your fifties and sixties, conservative in your seventies and up. Don't bother "diversifying" by buying both an aggressive fund and a conservative one. Taken together, that gives you a "moderate" mix, so you might as well put all your money into the moderate fund right from the start.

The three companies I've mentioned that offer target retirement funds also sell lifecycle funds. As usual, costs matter. You pay the least for Vanguard's four lifecycle funds, called "LifeStrategy Funds." (They're also based on indexed investing, discussed below.) Ascending the cost ladder, look at Fidelity's four "Asset Manager Funds." Then T. Rowe Price's three "Personal Strategy Funds."

For ease of use, lifecycle funds are my second choice. They require you to decide how much stock market risk you want to take (you may not necessarily know). Also, you have to pick the right time to switch from one fund to another. But they're simpler, by far, than trying to pick from an array of mystery funds. They're professionally diversified and you can hold them a long time. They're also regularly rebalanced, to keep your mix of stocks and bonds at the level you originally chose. Rebalancing is a key service that you'll read more about later. Lifecycle funds will give you better returns, and at less risk, than you'd probably earn from the random mix of stocks and funds you might otherwise buy yourself.

The Amazing Magic of Index Mutual Funds

Target retirement funds and lifecycle funds are still so new on the scene that only the most far-seeing retirement plans offer them. But it's becoming common for plans to own index funds, the third and last supersmart investment on my short list. With just a few index funds, you can create your own well-diversified portfolio, giving you growth for the future without exposing yourself to too much risk. Here's how index funds work and why they're so good.

To start with, what's an index? It's a way of measuring changes in price. You're probably familiar with the Consumer Price Index, which tells you how fast or slowly prices are rising for consumer goods. A stock market index tells you how fast stock prices are moving and whether they're going up or down. Was it a happy day in the market, a ho-hum day, or a rotten day? The index knows.

The stock market index that you hear the most about is the Dow Jones Industrial Average. The Dow covers 30 large American companies. The change in their average price shows whether the market was strong or weak that day. When the Dow rises, the talking heads on TV will intone that "stocks went up." When it falls, "stocks went down."

If you're an investor, however, other indexes matter more. The most important is Standard & Poor's 500 (the S&P 500, for short)—a composite of 500 leading U.S. companies. It contains many more stocks than the Dow, which makes it a superior way of tracking how well America's larger companies perform over time. The Wilshire 5000 index tracks the performance of smaller stocks as well as larger ones, so you get a picture of the total market, overall. Other indexes track the performance of bond prices, international stocks, and the stocks of certain industries such as real estate. You can see at a glance whether their prices are up, down, or flat.

What's an index mutual fund? It's an investment designed to copy the performance of a particular market index. The best example is the S&P 500. An S&P index fund owns the stocks of those 500 companies. When the index rises 5 percent, an S&P 500 index fund will also rise 5 percent (minus whatever the manager charges in fees). When you buy this fund, your money is invested in the average performance of America's major corporations.

There are index funds for many other markets, too. Some funds track the Wilshire 5000 index for large and small stocks. Some track only the smaller stocks. Some track international stocks. Some track specific industries, such as real estate, utilities, or energy. There are bond funds, too. Index funds are basically run by computer, which adjusts the fund's investments to match the way the market changed that day. Each fund does as well as its particular market overall.

How are index funds different from other mutual funds? All the other mutual funds are run by people, not by computer. They're called *actively managed funds* because managers decide which stocks or bonds to hold. One manager may love Cisco Systems, so he buys a lot of it. Another may load up on Procter & Gamble, which she thinks will do even better. Only in hindsight will you know which one was right.

Professionals try to "beat the market"—meaning beat the returns on index funds. Believing (or hoping) they'll succeed, investors pay them higher fees. That feels like the right way to invest. You assume that the people who study the market full time will produce superior results. But it's all mystique, as the dismal record shows. You're better off skipping managed funds and trusting your money to the magic of the market (that is, index funds) instead.

Can managed mutual funds beat index funds? They can, but on average they usually don't. It's *hard* to beat the performance of the total market over time. A particular fund may do better than the index for three years or five years. When you read that the Super Bucks Fund has been rising by 30 percent while the market averages just poked along, you rush to buy. But Super Bucks will almost certainly fall behind the market over the following three or five years—often by a lot. It soared because it happened to focus on an industry that suddenly got hot—telecom, energy, banks, whatever. When those stocks cool down, the fund will fall. With rare exceptions, top funds don't stay on top even with a talented manager at the helm. When you average their good years with their bad ones, they usually lag.

Countless studies have proved that point. Here's just one of them.* It compares the performance of large mutual funds ($100 million and up) run by professional money managers with the S&P 500 Index Fund run by the Vanguard Group:

- Over the 10 years ended in 1998, the 500 Index Fund beat the large managed funds by 3.5 percent a year (counting only the funds that lasted for the whole period). That's a huge difference. If you'd put $10,000 in each type of investment, your 500 Fund would have paid you $7,780 more. After federal taxes, the results were even worse. The 500 Index Fund beat the average manager by 4.5 percent a year for investors who cashed out—paying them $9,623 more. Indexers netted almost twice the money that managed-fund investors did.

---

* By Robert Arnott, Andrew Berkin, and Jia Ye, published in the *Journal of Portfolio Management*, Summer 2000.

- The results were similar over 15-year and 20-year periods. The index fund won, decisively. The results for managed funds would have been even worse if the study had subtracted the sales commission paid on funds sold by stockbrokers and planners.

- Some of the managed funds in the study did better than the Vanguard 500, but not by a lot. Furthermore, there's no way of spotting those outperformers in advance. The mutual fund you decide to buy (because it's hot today) will probably not be the one that tops the scoreboard a decade from now. In fact, in the 1989–98 period, the odds that an index fund would beat a managed fund were 6 to 1. If that were a horse, I'd bet my savings on it to win. In fact, I did. I've been betting on index funds ever since I discovered them, early in my investing life.

Managed-fund advocates argue that periods ended in 1998 uniquely favored index funds, so the results of this study don't count. They're wrong. You get similar results when you look at periods ended in other years. Over some five-year stretches, index funds run toward the middle of the pack, but once you reach 10 years they usually move to the upper quarter or higher. Remember, investing is a game of odds. You're not aiming for the top fund every year—that's an impossible goal. To be a winner, you simply need a fund that runs well above average, over the long term. That's what you can count on an index fund to do.

Every now and then a money manager has a streak. He or she might beat the market 10 years or more in a row. These prodigies attract exuberant attention, proving how rare a phenomenon they are. You don't know in advance who they're going to be, of course, so you may not discover them until they're several years into their game. By then, their streak will be closer to its end. Sometimes, managers win in little corners of the market, such as developing countries. But as a no-worry investor, you're not hunting for niches. You want a few broad funds that include the niche markets, too— and for broad funds, in particular, the indexers usually win.

Why do money managers lose, given all their resources and expertise? First, they can't guess—consistently—which stocks will beat the market. Second, they're always buying and selling, which runs up the brokerage expenses the fund has to pay. Third, their constant trading racks up taxable capital gains—another cost, if you hold the fund in a taxable account. Finally, they charge high fees. You *hope* they'll beat the market, which is why you pay. But in most years, you're paying them to fail! To be worth your time, a manager has to do well enough to match the investment return you'd get from an index fund, *plus* cover his or her extra costs, *plus* cover your extra taxes, *plus* give you a higher return on your money. Not very likely. Over time, you'll almost certainly beat them with a low-cost index fund.

What happens to index funds when the market drops? Index funds fall when the market does. Managed funds do, too. But index funds never sink further than the market, as so many growth funds and tech funds did during the long collapse of 2000 through 2002. The way to reduce your losses during the months when stocks turn down is *not* to bet that a manager will predict the downturn and outsmart it. That's a bad bet. Instead, use index funds to diversify. Own two or three different types of index funds, to provide yourself with some protection as well as growth. You'll see how to create your own investment mix later in this chapter.

If index funds usually beat managed funds, how come investors keep giving managed funds their money? Lots of reasons. The money managers talk a good game. They're the experts. You read admiring stories about them in personal-finance magazines— always the ones with terrific recent records (recent losers don't get interviewed). Managed funds advertise "top performance," and advertising works. You can't help believing that today's best funds will stay on top—the continuing triumph of hope over experience. Everyone else buys managed funds and you think they must know something. They're the funds that stockbrokers and most financial planners sell. When your hot fund cools, you assume you merely made a wrong pick and should look to another, better fund. That's what the experts say to do.

Money managers and financial salespeople laugh at index funds. They remind you that indexing gives you "average" performance and who wants to be just average? You want to do better, right? But most managed funds *don't* beat the average, over time, even though they claim they can. Think about Chico Marx in *Duck Soup*, saying, "Who are you going to believe, me or your own eyes?"

Believe your own eyes. The research on index funds is right.

What does "average" market performance really mean? In the normal world, "average" means "middle" (ugh, probably mediocre). But not in the investing world. When you're looking at market performance, "average" is actually "high": high returns over the long run, compared with your alternatives. The stock market average is like par in golf—the score that only the best players get. A few golfers beat par but most fall short. Money managers can sometimes beat the market over short terms, but over the long term, most fall short. If your investment performance matches the market average, you're up there with the very best.

Indexing can get frustrating if you watch the market all the time. You'll keep seeing funds that do better and think you should buy them, instead. There are periods when a third or more of the managed funds may be ahead. But decades of data prove that the market is hard to beat. The funds that outperformed during the past five years will be different from the winners in the period five years before. If you keep trying to catch the winners, you'll keep making mistakes (studies show this, too). Besides, you're *busy!* You want to ignore your investments while you live your life.

Twenty or 30 years from now, you want to wake up, look at the size of your retirement fund, and say, "Wow." Indexing is a wow.*

Which index funds should you buy? When two different funds are following the same index, the one with the lower costs will always perform the best. Vanguard, which invented the index fund for individuals, used to hold the low-cost crown and still does for smaller investments. At this writing, it's charging 0.18 percent a year for its most popular funds, on a minimum investment of $3,000 ($1,000 for an IRA). In 2004, however, Fidelity elbowed into Vanguard's business. It's now charging 0.10 percent a year for similar funds, on a $10,000 minimum investment.†

Several other mutual-fund families offer two or three index funds. But beware the costs! I've seen index funds charging 1 percent and more, which is a total rip-off.

For No Worry investing, the following are the only index funds you should be looking at. Later, I'll show you how to put them all together. I'm recommending just three fund families—Vanguard, Fidelity, and T. Rowe Price. T. Rowe Price is generally the most expensive of the three, but its fees are still low compared with the rest of the mutual-fund world. I'm also throwing in a wild card, for commodities.

1. *Funds that track the entire American stock market.* Fidelity's Spartan Total Market, Vanguard's Total Stock Market Index, or

---

* If you'd like to read more on the superiority of indexing and diversification, I have three books to recommend: *Winning the Loser's Game: Timeless Strategies for Successful Investing,* by the famous investment consultant Charles Ellis; *The Only Guide to a Winning Investment Strategy You'll Ever Need: The Way Smart Money Invests Today,* by Larry Swedroe of Buckingham Asset Management, which manages money for wealthy people; and *Unconventional Success: A Fundamental Approach to Personal Investment,* by David Swensen, who has made a spectacular success of managing Yale University's endowment.

† On $100,000 or more, Fidelity charges 0.07 percent. Vanguard charges 0.09 percent. Fees also are low for investors who have been with Vanguard at least 10 years and have at least $50,000 there. Always watch these prices; they could change.

T. Rowe Price's Total Equity Index. These are the most widely diversified U.S. stock funds you can buy, and my personal favorites. You are investing in the American economy as a whole.

2. *Funds for international stocks.* Every well-diversified investment plan should include some international stocks. You may think they're risky. But academic studies have proved that owning an international fund reduces your long-term risk and increases your returns. That may not happen in any particular year but it's true over many years. Your best choices: Fidelity Spartan International Fund, which invests in the leading companies in the industrialized world—Europe, Australia, and the Far East, principally Japan. Or Vanguard's Total International Stock Fund, which is even more diversified—investing in both the developed world and in the "emerging" markets of Eastern Europe, Southeast Asia, and Latin America. Or T. Rowe Price's International Equity Index, including some emerging markets.

3. *An index fund for real-estate diversification.* There's only one—Vanguard's REIT Index Fund ("REIT" mean real estate investment trust). REITs buy commercial real estate, such as shopping centers, apartment buildings, and hotels. They often do well when other stocks are doing poorly, so owning them reduces your total investment risk.

4. *Bond index funds.* Diversified bond funds invest in both government and corporate bonds. Look at Vanguard's Total Market Bond Index Fund, T. Rowe Price's U.S. Bond Index Fund, or Fidelity's U.S. Bond Index Fund. Investors own bonds to limit their risk. The younger you are, the less you need bonds (although, for diversification, you always need some).

5. *A commodities index fund.* "Commodities" covers agricultural and natural resources, such as oil, metals, timber, and grain. The mutual funds are expensive to own but an excellent hedge against inflation. In fact, this could be the sector that shines if stocks and bonds yield only modest returns over the next

several years. Few commodities funds exist for individual investors. I'd suggest only Pimco's Commodity Real Return Strategy Fund. It's linked to a popular commodities price index and also invests in government bonds whose returns are adjusted for inflation. Its price is out of my usual range; broker-sold shares cost as much as 1.99 percent a year in fees. Alternatively, you could open an account at a mutual-fund "supermarket," such as those offered by Charles Schwab & Co. or Fidelity Investments. They let you buy funds from many different companies through a single source. At a supermarket, Commodity Real Return costs 1.24 percent a year.

These five types of funds—U.S. stock, international stock, real estate, bond, and commodity—are all you need for a well-diversified investment plan. Vanguard has other index funds tracking all kinds of markets, but you could drive yourself crazy trying to choose among them. There's simply no point. The funds that I've been talking about will give you everything you need.

That said, I'll mention three more types of funds because they might interest you or your company might offer them in your retirement plan.

1. *Funds that track Standard & Poor's 500-stock index.* They cover America's 500 leading companies, which represent more than 70 percent of the U.S. stock market. Personally, I prefer a Total Market fund, which includes these companies and adds smaller ones, too. In many 401(k)s, however, the 500 fund may be the only stock index fund you can get—in which case, go for it. There's Fidelity Spartan 500 Index Fund, Vanguard's 500 Index Fund, and T. Rowe Price's Equity Index 500.

2. *Funds that track the performance of midsize and smaller stocks.* These stocks are also included in the Total Market funds that I prefer. But sometimes a 401(k) plan offers an S&P 500

fund and a small-stock fund separately. In that case, buy both. Look for Fidelity's Spartan Extended Market Fund, Vanguard's Extended Market Index Fund, or T. Rowe Price's Extended Equity Market Index Fund.

3. *A fund for socially conscious investors.* I like Vanguard Calvert Social Index Fund. It tracks the performance of about 600 large U.S. companies whose policies are considered favorable to workers, consumers, and the environment.

How to get two winning strategies for the price of one. Vanguard's target retirement funds and lifecycle funds both use indexing strategies to invest. You get the total-diversification advantage, plus market performance at low cost. The competing target and lifecycle funds, from Fidelity, T. Rowe Price, and other fund companies, rely on money managers to pick the stocks and bonds. Given the record, they'll have a tough time beating Vanguard's indexed approach. They might succeed, however, if their managed funds pick a mix of particularly good stocks or if they hold a higher percentage of stocks in the portfolio than Vanguard does.

Should you give up on managed funds entirely? Not if you like to play with investments or have some mutual funds you're happy with. Use target, lifestyle, or index funds as your main meal, with a small side dish of managed funds that interest you. If you fall out of love with a managed fund, however, don't replace it with another one. Take the hint and add to your core investments instead.

TAXES AND MUTUAL FUNDS

Taxes don't matter, if you're choosing investments in a 401(k), Individual Retirement Account, or other retirement plan. All your gains are tax-deferred until you take money out. With a Roth IRA (page 32), your gains are never taxed.

But if you're investing outside a retirement plan, taxes matter a lot. When your mutual fund earns taxable income, the tax is passed along to you.

You receive two forms of taxable income from mutual funds. First, income and dividends paid by the stocks and bonds the fund owns. Second, capital gains on securities that the fund sells at a profit.

In managed mutual funds, most managers constantly buy and sell stocks, which means that they stick you with a lot of taxable gains. By selling winners, they can generate taxes even in a year when the market value of the fund declines. That's insult and injury, combined! Some funds are "tax-managed," meaning that they manage their investments in ways that minimize this cost.

The broad index funds, such as Total Market and the S&P 500 funds, produce minimal taxable income because they don't trade stocks. As a result, you get a better return, after taxes, than you do from managed funds.

Target retirement funds and lifecycle funds generate some taxes, as they change your investments to keep your portfolio on track. But they're generally managed in a way that holds taxes down. You can minimize the tax even further by investing with Vanguard, which takes an indexing approach.

Investors often don't think about taxes when they buy a mutual fund. But you should. Taxes can be a heavy cost, and costs reduce your wealth.

HOW TO DIVERSIFY YOUR INVESTMENTS

Target retirement funds and lifecycle funds diversify your investments for you. That's why I like them so much. No muss, no fuss. But if you're investing through an account that doesn't offer these funds (an IRA or 401(k)), you'll have to diversify by yourself.

Diversifying your money does *not* mean owning a lot of different mutual funds. You could own 15 funds and not be diversified, if all those funds invest in similar stocks. That's what trapped so many investors when the stock market bubble burst. They'd bought a collection of high-performing "growth" funds, all of which concentrated on technology stocks. When the techs fell, they took these funds down with them. Investors had no idea how undiversified their money was, until the market showed them.

To be diversified means owning different *types* of investments that rise and fall at different times. For example, when stock prices fall, bond prices often rise. If you own them both, you're diversified. The rising value of your bonds cushions the loss you're taking on stocks. Together, they save you from taking too much risk.

Below, I've listed the major rules of diversification used by the managers of pension funds. It's easy for individuals to use them, too. Later, you'll see how to use these rules to create very simple yet well-balanced portfolios. Here's what you need to know:

1. Stocks behave differently from bonds. When stock prices are falling, bond prices usually go up (not always, but often enough). There have even been 10-year and 15-year periods when bonds did better than stocks, something that few investors realize. If you own only stocks, you are not diversified. *Rule 1: Own stocks and bonds.*

2. The stocks of different industries rise and fall at different times. Technology stocks may be going down while utility stocks are going up. *Rule 2: Use index funds, because they own the stocks of every industry.*

3. The stocks of smaller companies rise and fall at different rates than the stocks of larger companies do. If you buy only big-company stocks, you are not diversified. *Rule 3: Buy index funds that cover companies of every size.*

4. The stocks of foreign companies often rise and fall at different times from U.S. stocks. You are not diversified if you invest only in U.S. stocks. *Rule 4: Own an international index mutual fund.*

5. Real estate stocks often rise when the rest of the stock market is going down. *Rule 5: Own a real-estate mutual fund.*

6. Most bond mutual funds decline in value when inflation and interest rates rise. But you get some protection with the government bonds called TIPS (Treasury Inflation-Protected Securities). When rates rise because inflation does, the price of these bonds stays pretty much unchanged. *Rule 6: Buy a TIPS fund as well as a regular bond fund.* (For why TIPS are best used in tax-deferred retirement accounts, see the next page.)

7. Commodities such as gold, copper, oil, and wheat rise and fall at different times from stocks and bonds. That means buying a commodities mutual fund. Unfortunately, it costs a lot to buy them. *Rule 7: Don't buy high-cost mutual funds except in unusual circumstances.* An indexed commodity diversification passes the test.

8. A single company can get into serious trouble even when other companies are doing fine. Take Enron and WorldCom, both frauds. Take Polaroid, bankrupted by new technology. *Rule 8: Never concentrate your investments in a single company, especially the company you work for.*

These rules don't work in every market all the time. But over a whole market cycle, they'll behave as advertised.

Diversification doesn't necessarily win you higher investment returns. It achieves something far more important: It reduces your risk. Your total investment pot (your "portfolio") won't fall as far in bad markets as other people's will, which leaves you in a far safer position. You'll feel better psychologically—less apt to panic and sell. And you're better prepared for the unforeseen, whatever that may be.

Three Tips on Bond Diversification

The simplest way to invest in bonds is through a Total Bond fund, which I've used in my sample portfolios beginning on page 180. You get diversification and some protection from risk. But I want to give you three other ideas, for different circumstances. You can ignore these suggestions but I'd be remiss if I didn't mention them.

1. *If you want to be super-safe.* Instead of a Total Bond fund, choose a fund that invests entirely in U.S. Treasury securities. Treasury funds don't pay as much interest as Total Bond funds do. But in a financial crisis, investors would flock to Treasuries. They could do well while corporate bonds decline. In short, they're a belt-and-suspenders bond investment, just in case.

2. *If you're investing through an IRA where taxes are deferred.* Choose a TIPS fund as part of your bond investment. TIPS stands for Treasury Inflation-Protected Securities. They're government bonds whose interest rate is adjusted for price inflation every year. If inflation rises, they pay more interest. If inflation falls, they pay less. In either case, they preserve your purchasing power, which ordinary bonds do not. There's just one technical hitch. The adjustment you get for inflation is treated as current, taxable income, but you don't get the money until you cash in the fund. For this reason, TIPS are best for tax-deferred accounts. Vanguard's TIPS fund costs 0.17 percent. T. Rowe Price's costs 0.5 percent. Fidelity's costs 0.63 percent.

3. *If you're investing outside a retirement plan and are in the 25 percent tax bracket or up.* Choose a tax-free municipal bond

fund. There are total U.S. funds and separate funds for various states. At Fidelity, you'll find funds for Arizona, California, Connecticut, Florida, Maryland, Massachusetts, Michigan, Minnesota, New Jersey, New York, Ohio, and Pennslyvania. At T. Rowe Price, funds for California, Florida, Georgia, Maryland, New Jersey, New York, and Virginia. At Vanguard, funds for California, Massachusetts, New Jersey, New York, Ohio, and Pennsylvania.

YOUR PERSONAL INVESTMENT MIX FOR LONG-TERM GROWTH

So much for the rules. How should you actually diversify your money? You need a plan.

The plans I'm showing here are designed for long-term investors who want to build a large enough fund to make themselves financially free. I've worked almost entirely with index funds. The allocations—drawn from conversations with top professionals—capture the stock market's superior growth and also limit your risk. They aren't set in stone, but offer you a sensible framework.

Vanguard is the only group that offers an indexed real-estate fund, costing 0.21 percent. You get real estate stocks in all the S&P 500 and Total Market funds, so when you add a separate fund, you are giving this sector extra weight.

For investors with retirement funds, including IRAs, I've included a fund for Treasury Inflation-Protected Securities (TIPS). If you don't use the TIPS fund, add that money to Total Bond.

Don't ignore the international fund. It will serve you well, long-term.

The Long-Term Growth Portfolio: Vanguard

U.S. Total Stock Market Index Fund	40%
Total International Stock Index Fund	20%
REIT (real estate) Index Fund	10%
Total Market Bond Index Fund	20%
Treasury Inflation-Protected Bond Fund	10%

Both Fidelity and T. Rowe Price have all the same pieces, except for the real-estate index fund. They do have managed real estate funds at a higher cost—Fidelity's Real Estate Investment Portfolio, at 0.85 percent; or T. Rowe Price's Real Estate Fund, at 0.9 percent. If you decide to put 10 percent of your money there, reduce your Total Market allocation to 40 percent. Again, if you don't use the TIPS fund, add that money to your Total Bond investment.

The Long-Term Growth Portfolio: Fidelity

Spartan Total Market Fund	50%
Spartan International Fund	20%
U.S. Bond Index Fund	20%
Fidelity Inflation-Protected Bond Fund	10%

The Long-Term Growth Portfolio: T. Rowe Price

Total Equity Index Fund	50%
International Equity Index Fund	20%
U.S. Bond Index Fund	20%
Inflation-Protected Bond Fund	10%

The Wild Card: Commodities

Pimco Commodity Real Return Strategy	5–10%

If you invest in Pimco's fund, take half the money from your Total Stock Market allocation and half from your Total Bond allocation. But invest only through a tax-deferred retirement account. Otherwise, this fund's investment strategy could sock you with a serious tax bill.

The Charles Schwab brokerage firm offers funds that track its own indexes. Schwab charges higher fees than Vanguard or Fidelity. But if you're a Schwab investor, they offer easy diversification. Use the same allocation as the one shown for Fidelity funds.

TIAA-CREF, the pension fund for those who work in academic, medical, cultural, and research fields, offers low-cost funds to individuals. There's a total market fund called Equity Index, costing 0.26 percent a year, but the rest of its funds aren't indexed.

Several other mutual-fund groups have index funds, especially for big-company and international stocks. But remember: Every fund that tracks the same index gets exactly the same investment result, minus fees. The higher the fee, the poorer your return. When choosing from a shelf of products, all alike, no one would knowingly take the most expensive one. Always check fees before you buy.

Finding the happiest possible investment mix. What if the investments I've suggested make you uncomfortable in some way? Just because the top pros consider them good picks doesn't make them right for everyone. You should change anything that really bothers you.

For example, some investors might not feel comfortable with so much in stock. If so, reduce the amount. Some of you might mistrust international investments. If so, throw them out. Over the long run, portfolios do better with more in stocks and with an international fund. But if you hate them, you'll sell the first time they drop in price—so owning them simply sets you up for a future loss. A fully diversified portfolio will reduce your total risk, but only when it's a mix of investments that you're willing to keep.

Don't throw out bonds, by the way, just because you're young and think that they're only for grandmothers. Bonds are valuable. They protect some of your money from loss and, in some years, actually do better than stocks.

Always think "portfolio." That means treating all your investments as a single money pot. People tend to put their assets into different mental compartments. If your stock funds drop 20 percent in price, you say, "Yikes, that's too much, I'd better sell." But your bond investments might be up. Counting them both together (that's your "portfolio"), your total investments may be down only 5 percent. That's a whole lot less scary. You can live with that small a loss while waiting for stocks to rise again. One of the great advantages of target retirement and lifecycle funds is that they're a portfolio in themselves.

Your marital portfolio. Husbands and wives often own separate pots of money—two 401(k)s, two IRAs, or maybe an inheritance held in just one name. If each of you makes a separate decision about diversification, your combined investments might not make sense. Instead, treat your assets as if they were all in a single fund. If one of you feels emotionally drawn to conservative bond investments, the other should consider putting more into stocks. Together, you'll come out in the middle. (This kind of mutual thinking assumes that you intend to stay married, of course!)

You've probably noticed that I've said practically nothing about mutual fund performance. Chasing top-performing funds is a loser's game. For proof, look at the annual studies of the "most popular" and "least popular" funds, done by the famous fund-research company, Morningstar. Almost always, the *least* popular funds turn out to be the best performers over the following three years. The popular ones fall to the bottom of the pack.

As a perfect example, take the recent history of technology funds. In the late 1980s, tech stocks were unloved and unbought. They exploded into life in the mid-1990s and peaked as the century turned, by which point people were in a frenzy to own them. Then they collapsed, taking investors' imaginary fortunes with them. Meanwhile, during the 1990s, international stocks were unloved and unbought. By 2005 they'd turned into the market's stars.

That won't last, of course. By the time you read this, something else will be big. Each type of stock has its day in the sun and then retreats. You imagine that your fund will pick techs (or whatever) when they're cheap, sell them at their peak, and jump right into the next big thing. That almost never happens. Mutual-fund managers stick with the universe of stocks they know.

Nevertheless, the vast herd of investors keeps on buying the popular mutual funds. They follow Morningstar's fund-rating system—five stars for the funds with the best risk-adjusted performance over the past 3, 5, and 10 years, four stars for the next best, and so on down the line. The funds are grouped by investment categories. Money pours into the starriest funds in the categories perceived as "hot." They're the only ones you see advertised—and they're also the funds most likely to disappoint.

Meanwhile, index funds continue their steady course. They own all types of stocks—the hot stocks that will be cold tomorrow and the cold stocks that will soon get hot. I have no idea which stocks will outperform three years from now and money managers don't know, either. But I know this: Whatever the leading companies are, the index funds will own them.

REBALANCING: THE SECRET INGREDIENT OF SUCCESS

Rebalancing is a mystery to most investors. You probably haven't heard of it or think it doesn't matter much. But it matters a lot. Rebalancing helps you limit your risk. One of the reasons to pick a target retirement or lifecycle fund is that it does the rebalancing for you and you don't have to bother learning what it is.

When you pick separate index funds, however, you have to re-balance them yourself. So here goes:

To "rebalance" means to keep your investment portfolio on an even keel. You want to hold roughly the same percentage of your money in stocks no matter what the market does. That keeps your account from getting either too risky or too conservative. You're aiming for a steady course.

To start the process, you have to decide what your "balance" should be—how much in stocks and how much in bonds. As a simple example, assume an account that's 70 percent invested in a stock index fund and 30 percent in a bond index fund. That's your home base.

As market prices change, however, the ratio of stocks to bonds will change as well. If stocks zoom up, they might soon account for 80 percent of the value of your investment portfolio. You'll feel rich, but you're also in a riskier position. If the rally fails, you have more to lose. So you rebalance. You sell some of your stock fund (at a profit) and put the proceeds into your bond fund. That brings you back to your original 70–30 split between stocks and bonds.

The next year, stocks might do poorly—dropping in value to only 60 percent of your portfolio. Your investments have now be-come too conservative, with too little money invested for growth. This time, you'd sell bonds and reinvest the proceeds in stocks, to raise your stock allocation back to 70 percent.

You handle all the types of investments you own in the same way. If you start with 20 percent in an international fund, and price changes raise its value to 25 percent of your money, you'd sell some of the shares to bring it back down to 20 percent and reinvest the proceeds in your U.S. stocks or bonds.

There's no need to rebalance after every little wiggle in the stock market. Do it only if one investment misses its home-base tar-get by more than 5 percent, up or down. Check your investments after any major rally (or once a year), to see if you should act.

Rebalancing makes you a smart investor. You sell at high prices (taking profits) and reinvest in lower-priced assets that haven't done as well. Those weaker performers will eventually go up and you'll make money because you bought them cheap. Remember: The types of assets that were yesterday's losers will be tomorrow's winners. A faithful rebalancer buys tomorrow's winners, automatically.

How do you rebalance? That depends on where the money is.

1. In a tax-deferred retirement account such as a 401(k) or IRA, rebalancing is easy. You'd sell some of the shares you hold in the investment that went up and reinvest the proceeds in investments that lagged. You might be able to make the changes yourself online. Or call the plan's customer service center. No taxes or penalties are involved. You might even find that there's online or personal help with making your rebalancing calculations.

2. If you're investing outside a retirement fund, you should handle rebalancing in a different way. You don't want to sell investments that rise in value because you'll owe taxes on the gain. So leave them alone and rebalance by adding extra money to the assets that fell behind. As an example, say you've been putting $200 a month into your investment account—$140 into a stock index fund and $60 into a bond fund, for a 70–30 split between stocks and bonds. After a good year, your stocks are now worth 80 percent of your portfolio. To bring your investments back into balance, start adding the whole $200 a month to your bond fund, until its value rises back to 30 percent of your total investment.

If you keep track of your finances with the latest versions of Quicken and Microsoft Money, you can get help with these calculations. Both products offer rebalancing programs that will tell you instantly whether you ought to sell and buy, and if so, how much.

My Rebalancing Sermon

I've been saying, over and over, that smart investing is easy. Rebalancing is the only thing that's hard—not hard mechanically but hard psychologically. You're selling stocks as their price goes up, when your every impulse is to hold or buy. If prices keep going up, you'll kick yourself for selling "too soon." The opposite happens on the downside. When stocks decline, you're supposed to buy. If you get scared and sell instead, you won't get the long-term advantage that this strategy brings.

Rebalancing takes discipline and courage. The only way to stand the strain is to hold a really deep belief that rebalancing works. To reinforce your belief, remember the stock market bubble. Wouldn't it have been nice if you'd sold some stocks when prices went sky-high? Wouldn't it have been nice to reinvest in bonds, which rose in value during the years that stocks collapsed? That's what rebalancing does. It works in every stock market cycle, all the time.

To prepare for your new rebalancing life, you have to do two things: (1) Decide on the percentage of stocks and bonds you want in your own portfolio, so you'll know what you're rebalancing *to*. (2) Use index funds, because they're the simplest things to rebalance with. It's hard to rebalance properly when you own a mix of managed funds and downright impossible when you own individual stocks.

HOW TO MANAGE A 401(K)

So much for the best investment strategies. How do you apply them to a 401(k) and similar retirement plans? Everything depends on what's offered. Some plans give you excellent choices while oth-

ers have poor ones. Some provide so many choices that you don't
know where to start. The more funds in your plan, the greater the
chance that you'll wind up with an unsuitable mix. Here's how to
work your way through it.

Two No-Brainers

1. If your plan offers a target retirement fund, switch all your
   money out of the other funds you've chosen and put it there.
   Pick the fund with the most plausible retirement date. It
   doesn't matter that you expect to leave the company well before retirement. A target fund will always be invested appro-
   priately for your age.
2. If your plan doesn't have a target retirement fund, see if it
   has a lifecycle fund and put all your money there. Think
   about whether you want an aggressive, moderate, or conservative mix.

Best Choices When Picking Other Mutual Funds

Here are some guidelines to start with, when you're investing for
the long term. Use index funds, if your plan offers them. A Total
Market fund can cover your big-stock and small-stock investment
combined. If index funds aren't on the menu, read the descriptions
of the plan's funds carefully. Choose the ones that best fit the descriptions below. Some funds buy "growth stocks," but that's only
half of the stock-owning universe (companies whose earnings are
growing fast). The other half are "value stocks" (companies whose
prices have been beaten down; usually excellent buys, over the long
run). You want a fund that buys both growth and value—in other
words, everything. Once a year, rebalance your investments back

to their original percentages. If your company doesn't offer a fund for international or real estate stocks, buy them outside your plan.

A GUIDELINE PORTFOLIO FOR 401(k)s

A diversified stock fund that owns big companies	35%
A diversified stock fund that owns smaller companies	15%
An international fund*	20%
A diversified bond fund	30%

* If there's no international fund, split your 401(k) money between the big-stock and small-stock fund.

Buying 401(k) advice. Increasingly, 401(k) plans are giving you access to personal investment advice. Sometimes it's online. Sometimes there's a call center where you can speak to an adviser and ask questions. The newest wrinkle is the 401(k) managed account. You get a personal manager who not only picks your mutual funds but also rebalances your investments automatically. You have to pay for the account, so it reduces your returns. But it's worth it, if you'll get better funds with lower risk.

Managing 401(k) plans that give you a poor choice of funds. Consider investing just enough to get the full employer match, if there is one. Invest the rest of your retirement money in a Roth IRA (page 32), outside the plan. One caveat: If you won't make regular, automatic contributions to the Roth IRA, it's better to stay with your employer plan, choosing its most diversified funds. The *saving* is the important part, and payroll deduction always works.

Increasing your contribution to your 401(k). You might start small, contributing maybe 5 percent of your paycheck each time, but get off that baby plan as fast as you can.

Start by finding out how much of your contribution (if any) your company will match. A match is free money; for every dollar you put up, your employer will add 50 cents or a dollar to your account up to a maximum amount. Contribute at least enough to collect the maximum. After that, start raising your contribution even further, until you're putting in as much as you're allowed. The best plans let you sign up for automatic increases in your contributions, usually occurring around the time you expect a raise.

If you haven't increased your 401(k) contribution lately, do it now. Inertia is one of investing's greatest enemies. You start with a certain percentage or dollar amount and you never get around to changing it. The same is true for investors in other types of retirement plans, such as IRAs. You can afford it, you just have to make the move.

Company stock in 401(k)s. Owning a lot of company stock is a huge risk. It doesn't matter that the stock has been going up. At some point it will fall, and the slide might occur just when you're getting ready to leave the company or retire. Some companies fail—witness Enron and WorldCom. Some sink into a long funk. If you say to yourself, "That can't happen to my wonderful company," you're relying on magic. Your company may indeed be wonderful but it can stumble all the same. Or the company can do well but the stock can stumble. You shouldn't have a ton of money in *any* single stock, but especially the stock of the company you work for.

If your employer matches your contribution with company stock, sell the stock as soon as you can and diversify into mutual funds. If you're not allowed to diversify, your bosses are rats. You can tell them I said so. They're lining their own pockets without giving a thought to the financial security of the rest of the people who work there. You should still take the match. Free stock is better than a poke in the eye, even if you can't diversify. The odds are good that its price will rise over the long run. But ignore it for retirement purposes. Invest the rest of your money as if it's all you have.

What about using your own contribution to buy company stock?

Go ahead, if you can buy at a discount and resell right away. Otherwise, skip it. If you can't resist holding some of the stock, never let it amount to more than 5 percent of your retirement plan. You never want to depend on your company for both your job and your retirement money.

Retirement-plan advice on the Web. My favorite site is Financialengines.com. Users enter a few bits of personal information, such as when you expect to retire, how much retirement income you'll need, and the level of risk you're willing to take (from "very conservative" to "very aggressive"). Then you enter the funds your plan offers and how much you're contributing now. Financial Engines will tell you whether your current strategy is likely to meet your retirement goal. If not, you'll get specific advice on what to change—how much more to save, how much longer you might have to work, and which mix of mutual funds would be a better choice. The cost, at this writing: $39.95 for a single assessment and $149.95 a year for continual monitoring. The advice is unbiased and independent. Financial Engines also takes into consideration any company stock you hold in your 401(k).

When you leave the plan because you're going to another job. Hang on to every penny in your retirement account. Don't take any money out and spend it. You'll pay taxes on your withdrawals, plus a 10 percent penalty if you're under 59½. Worse, you'll be stunting the growth of the nest egg you're going to need when you retire. Even small amounts, such as $5,000, will grow into a substantial sum over 30 years. So roll your plan money—all of it—into an Individual Retirement Account. Choose one at a mutual-fund company that offers the kinds of funds that you've read about here. To avoid taxes on the switch, the money has to be transferred directly to the IRA from your 401(k). The fund company's customer service line will tell you how.

HOW TO MANAGE A 403(B)

These plans are typically offered to public school teachers, among others. I approach them with a heavy heart. You should definitely participate; they're payroll-deductible and tax-deferred. But school districts tend to offer these plans through insurance agents, whose mutual funds and annuities cost two or three times as much as the funds in 401(k)s. It's dereliction of duty; you ought to scream to the school board and administrators. There's no excuse for sticking teachers with poorer plans than corporate employees have. Hospital 403(b)s often have better options, too.

If you're among the stuck, however, here's what to do.

Get the list of the investment plans your school district uses (called the vendor list) from your school office. If it includes low-cost groups such as Vanguard and TIAA-CREF, or Fidelity, T. Rowe Price, and USAA, you're in luck. Get the enrollment forms and sign up for the plan yourself. You don't need a salesperson as intermediary. Use the diversification rules you've seen above to choose your mutual funds.

If you're forced to invest through an insurance agent, choose the insurer's mutual funds rather than its annuities (for annuities, see page 201). Agents push the annuities because they pay much higher commissions. But their high costs mean poorer investment returns. Also, you usually can't change investments until six or seven years have passed, making it difficult to rebalance. The agents who sell you 403(b)s will probably present themselves as "financial advisers," eager to help you decide on the best ways to invest. Always remember: They're salespeople, that's all. For good advice on 403(b)s, see 403bwise.com.

HOW TO MANAGE AN
INDIVIDUAL RETIREMENT ACCOUNT

This one's easy. Just follow the do-it-yourself advice that starts on page 30. You may decide that you need a new IRA to get the mutual funds you want. You can roll money from your old IRA into your new one, tax-free. Your new plan will handle the paperwork.

PUTTING IT ALL TOGETHER

From the start of this book, you've been planning to arrange your money in a better way. Here's where it finally happens. There's a logical investment for each of your personal goals.

To find it, start by jotting down your reasons to save and invest. There aren't many categories—probably Debt Repayment, Ready Cash, Vacation, Down Payment for a Home, College, Starting a Business, Retirement—the kinds of things we've talked about so far.

Next to each category, specify roughly when you'll need the money. Right now? Within five years or less? Five to 10 years? More than 10 years? As you start looking further ahead you can't know for sure, but give it your best guess.

Once you've listed the goal and the time frame, the right type of investment falls into place automatically.

- *Money you'll need right now* or that has to be on hand belongs in a bank account or money-market mutual fund.
- *Money you'll need within five years* could stay in a money-market fund or a bank certificate of deposit. If you're familiar with bond investing, you might choose a short-term bond mutual fund (all the fund groups have them). These funds yield

more than certificates of deposit but they rise and fall a little in price, depending on market conditions. You're taking the risk of losing a small amount of money in hopes of making more than your bank will pay. In general, it's a pretty good bet. Do *not* put short-term money into the stock market. Over five-year periods, stock prices can fall and not come back, as we learned after the 2000 stock collapse. If you're really going to need this money, it never should be at serious risk.

- *Money you'll need in 5 to 10 years* could go into bond index mutual funds. Don't make vague guesses about the expenses you might have during this time frame. Put down only what you know—for example, college tuition for a child who's currently 12, or development costs for a business you intend to start. Bond index funds yield more than you'd get from a short-term bond fund. They also rise and fall more in price, which is something you have to be prepared for. But bonds aren't as risky as stocks, so you can be more certain that you'll have this money when you want it.

- *Money you won't need for 10 years or more* can go into broad-based mutual funds that invest primarily in stocks: target retirement funds, lifecycle funds, or a well-chosen portfolio of index funds.

With this in mind, fill in the table on the next page. The first two columns show your goals and when you're likely to need the money. The third column gives you the right investments for each purpose, based on the time frame you picked.

Next, pick up that list you made of all the investments you have now. (Remember that? Back in Chapter 1?) They go into the fourth column. Match each investment to the reason for having it, and compare it with the "right investments" in column three. Columns three and four should agree. Are you building a Cushion Fund in a money market account? Good, just right. Do you own a growth-stock mutual fund to help pay tuition for a child who'll be going to college in three years? Oops, you're taking too much risk. The time frame tells you to put that tuition money into short-term bonds and cash. Circle the sum, as a reminder to move it.

Finally, list the long-term investments that you hope to retire on someday and compare them with the funds in the No Worry plan. If they don't look suitable anymore, circle them, too. If you're just beginning to invest, you'll have a blank sheet—ready for a No Worry plan right from the start.

Your outline will look something like the table below.

Now, go back one more time to that list of investments you

What I Need Money For	When I'll Need It	The Right Investments	Where the Money Is Now	How Much I've Saved	Monthly Addition
Debt Repayment	Right Now	Bank account	_____	$_____	$_____
Cushion Fund	Anytime	Bank account or money-market fund	_____	$_____	$_____
Vacation	In 6 months	Bank account or money-market fund	_____	$_____	$_____
Starting a business	In 5 years	Money-market fund or short-term bond fund	_____	$_____	$_____
College, Amy	In 7 years	Bond funds, in a college savings plan	_____	$_____	$_____
College, Jim	In 12 years	Stock funds and bond funds in a college savings plan	_____	$_____	$_____
Retirement	In 30 years	Funds for both stocks and bonds with the majority in stocks	_____	$_____	$_____
Other	_____	_____	_____	$_____	$_____

made in Chapter 1. You weren't always sure why you'd chosen each particular one. Why this fund and not that one, why those particular stocks? Maybe you saw a mutual-fund ad claiming "top performance" or talked to a stockbroker who said that he'd take care of everything. Maybe you asked someone at work what she did with her 401(k), and copied that. We're all subject to these kinds of influences and follow them with our fingers crossed. But they don't help you stick to your course, let alone understand what you're doing. You could be swept into something else by another ad from a newer fund or a stockbroker's confident chat. *That's* why you worry— you're not sure whether you're doing things right.

With the No Worry plan, you know exactly why you've made each choice. One fund for growth, one fund to limit risk, one fund for international diversification, one fund for a real-estate hedge, all of them for their diversification and low costs. Having a *reason* for owning something—one that's well thought out—protects you from Wall Street's noise. You can tell at a glance that the stuff being hyped doesn't fit into your plan. Keep your new list of investments in your personal file, along with written notes on why you own each one.

CHANGING YOUR INVESTMENTS: STARTING FRESH

If you're just starting to invest, it's easy to set up a No Worry plan. Just pick the sensible mutual funds and contribute regularly.

If you're in a 401(k) it's easy, too. Choose a new fund (or funds) for yourself and switch your money there. Plans have call centers, or you may be able to handle the change yourself, online.

If you're in an Individual Retirement Account, look at all the mutual funds available. Switch to the types of funds that fit a No Worry plan. If you can't find any, open an IRA with a better mutual-fund group. You can roll money, tax-free, out of your old IRA and into a new one. The new plan will tell you how. It's also smart to consolidate your IRAs so you don't have to keep track of a lot of separate accounts. If you bought your old IRA through a bank, insurance company, or brokerage firm, there may be a penalty for switching before five or six years have passed. In that case, open an IRA for new contributions and move the old money when the penalty period ends.

If you're investing in a taxable account—that is, an account that's not in a retirement plan—you'll have to consider taxes before switching your investments around. You'll owe a capital gains tax if you sell shares at a profit, and taxes diminish the size of your investment pot. There are three things to do:

1. Swallow the taxes and move to something that's better for you, especially if the amounts of money are small and your old funds have been poor performers. Spring-clean your portfolio. Get rid of all those hangers-on. *Or* . . .

2. Check your investments—your stocks and mutual funds—to see if any of them have lost money since the day you bought. Sell the losers. At the same time, sell one or more of your winning funds. The tax law lets you reduce your gains by the amount of your loss, so you may owe little or no tax. Reinvest the proceeds in No Worry funds. *Or* . . .

3. Leave your old funds alone and start a target retirement or life-cycle fund with the new money you're investing regularly. Your investments won't be well balanced, at first, because of the drag from the older funds. But as the years pass, the newer funds will dominate.

If you have a taxable account plus a retirement account, think of them as a single pot. Do all the rebalancing in your tax-deferred plan. For example, say that the value of the stocks in both accounts went up. You'd leave your taxable account alone but sell double the amount in your tax-deferred account. That brings your total investment pot back into balance without your having to pay a tax.

WHAT ARE YOUR ALTERNATIVES TO THE NO WORRY PLAN?

Frankly, your alternatives aren't good. They're high-cost, poorly diversified, and don't do as well as low-cost index funds. Why do people choose them? Because they have no idea how well (or poorly) their investments are really faring compared with the market as a whole. If the value of their account goes up or they get a windfall in a single stock, they say, "I have a wonderful stockbroker." They don't realize that the broker probably hasn't performed as well as a simple Total Market index fund. Academic studies show that, as investors, we tend to think we've done better than is actually the case. That's what keeps all the useless parts of the investment industry alive.

THE CASE AGAINST BUYING INDIVIDUAL STOCKS

As a long-term investor, you might think that your job is to find "great companies" and hold their stocks forever. Legendary investors such as Warren Buffett say that's the right idea. But Buffett buys substantial stakes in corporations and has something to say about running them. The rest of us watch from the sidelines, where it's clear that "great companies" don't necessarily last. The superstars of 1990 were has-beens by 2000. The leaders in 2000 soon saw their stocks collapse. In hindsight, you can always find stocks with wonderful long-term records. But you can't know in advance which ones they're going to be.

You take big risks when buying individual stocks. Here's a short list:

1. *You overpay.* A stock price is supposed to reflect the company's expected growth in future earnings and dividends. But when stocks are popular, people bid up their prices to unrealistic levels. In the late 1990s, tech stocks were selling for far more than they could ever deliver in earnings growth. Investors kept buying, based on the theory of the "greater fool" (as in, "I may be a fool to pay this high price but I'll sell it to a greater fool who will pay even more"). Prices collapsed when the last fool decided not to play. Microsoft was and is a great company, but in 1999, it definitely wasn't a great stock.

2. *You buy stocks in the news.* That's where you hear about companies—and, of course, so does everyone else. Newsy stocks are more apt to be overpriced, compared with companies you've never heard of. You only hear about underpriced stocks after they've risen 50 percent (and they're newly in the news!). Stockbrokers like to sell newsy stocks because those are the ones you're mostly likely to be interested in.

3. *You buy and hold.* That's what long-term investors are supposed to do. But business moves too fast today. Only a very few companies turn in splendid long-term results—mostly those in traditional businesses and paying dividends.* Others bite the dust. To keep a portfolio of good stocks you have to weed them constantly—selling some and buying others. But even professionals can't do that well. And neither can you or I.

4. *You don't know—and cannot know—what's going on in a company.* If you own an individual stock, take this little test: How

---

* The 20 top performers in Standard & Poor's 500 Index, for 1957–2003, from *The Future for Investors* by Jeremy Siegel: Altria (formerly Philip Morris), Abbot Laboratories, Bristol-Myers Squibb, Tootsie Roll Industries, Pfizer, Coca-Cola, Merck, PepsiCo, Colgate-Palmolive, Crane, H. J. Heinz, Wrigley, Fortune Brands, Kroger, Schering-Plough, Procter & Gamble, Hershey Foods, Wyeth, Royal Dutch Petroleum, and General Mills. These aren't investment recommendations. Some companies on this list have had troubles, too. But notice that there's not a tech stock in the bunch. Each generation's tech stocks got blown away by something new.

good is the business? What are the trends in profit margins, sales rates, and inventories? How competent are its top executives, what are their problems, and how are they handling them? Is the market share rising or falling in the company's various lines of business? What's the competition up to, at home and abroad? You probably can't answer these questions and there's no reason you should. Without answers, however, you have no basis for deciding whether to buy, hold, or sell the stock. After the once-lordly Lucent tumbled, we discovered that it had made a wrong bet on fiber-optics technology and its management was a mess. Who knew, until we read it in the newspapers and the stock was down 90 percent?

5. *You don't diversify.* To be properly diversified, you'd have to hold 50 or more stocks in various industries and in companies of different sizes. Individuals can't do that. You hold just a few stocks, in popular companies. If one of those companies goes bad, it's hard to recover.

6. *You have no idea how well your total stock portfolio has performed.* Typically, you remember your winners, every single one of them. You forget your losers. You never average the two together. So you have no idea whether you've done as well as the market, over time. Almost certainly, you're behind.

Stocks have an entertainment value, for people who like the game and have time on their hands. It's exciting to see a stock go up (I won't mention the down). If you love to play, set aside 5 percent of your investment fund and cheerio. But do yourself and your family a favor and keep your long-term, life-changing money in well-diversified mutual funds.

THE CASE AGAINST WORKING WITH STOCKBROKERS

There actually aren't any "stockbrokers" anymore. They call themselves "financial consultants," "financial advisers," "planners," or "vice presidents." But they're still salespeople, which means that their interests are very different from yours. To make a living and keep their jobs, they have to get you to buy something. They lean toward the products that carry the highest fees. As the recent Wall Street scandals show, brokerage firms may give you tainted advice in order to make more money for themselves. Good brokers try to balance those interests by making money for you both. Bad brokers happily sell you bad stuff because that's what pays them the highest commissions. Either type costs you money. Why do you think that brokerage firms don't show your annual performance on your year-end statements? They don't want you to know.

Brokers rationalize the expense by saying that, if you need advice, you have to expect to pay for it. I agree. The question is whether you're getting "advice" or just the illusion of advice. Brokers dream of becoming "top producers"—meaning "producers of sales commissions." That wins them plaques, free trips to expensive vacation spots, gifts, bonuses, and all the other trappings of success. They're trained to sound like investment advisers but their real job is closing the deal—selling the sizzle, not the steak. Nice as they are, you're their livelihood, not their friend.

Here are some of the things brokers love (but you should avoid):

- *Individual stocks.* I've already talked about the uselessness of trying to pick stocks yourself. Brokers don't do any better. They have stacks of information, from analysts who produce lists of stocks to "buy," "hold," or "sell." But there's no guarantee that you, or they, will pick the winners from that list. And all the other risks remain—paying too much, holding too long, not diversifying.

- *Wrap accounts or managed accounts.* You give the broker your money. He or she invests it with professional managers or mutual funds. For "advice" and "oversight," the broker charges 1.5 percent or more. The managers also charge a fee. And what do you have in the end? Nothing more than the rough equivalent of a lifecycle mutual fund, except that you've paid 10 times more for it than necessary.

- *Tax-deferred annuities.* These investments just slay me (and will slay your retirement funds, too). They're managed mutual funds tucked into an insurance product. That allows them to grow tax-deferred. Investors love terms like "tax-deferred" because they assume they're saving money. In this case, *not.* Broker-sold annuities are a hugely expensive way of buying mutual funds. You pay higher fees than if you bought those same funds outside the annuity, so your performance suffers. There are penalties if you withdraw the money before seven years or more have passed. And you'll pay higher taxes on the gains when you eventually cash your annuity in.

  Annuities generally guarantee that your investment will always be worth at least what you paid. But the cost of that guarantee is high (meaning poorer performance compared with regular mutual funds). You probably won't even need it if you plan to hold for the long term. Tax-deferred annuities are one of the highest-commission products that brokers, insurance agents, and commission-based planners have to sell, which explains why they "encourage" you to buy. This business is also plagued with deceptive sales.

- *Managed mutual funds.* I've already explained that actively managed mutual funds rarely beat index funds, over time. The funds sold by brokers are especially poor. To see why, you need to know more about the fees that mutual funds charge.

Mutual funds fall into two broad categories, depending on their sales charges or *loads*.

No-load funds—with no sales charges—are sold by the fund companies themselves. You buy them by calling the fund directly or downloading their account registration forms online. You can sell without penalty whenever you want (sometimes there's a short waiting period before you can sell, of about 30 to 90 days).

Salespeople sell *load funds*—funds with sales charges. There are various types of load-fund shares, each with its own set of expenses. "A shares" carry an upfront sales commission (usually around 4.5 percent) plus an annual marketing fee called a *12(b)1 fee.* "B shares" and "C shares" charge nothing upfront but levy higher 12(b)1s. If you sell B or C shares within five or six years, you pay a penalty called a *contingent deferred sales charge* or *back-end load.* That's a lotta money out the door. (Tip for people who work with stockbrokers anyway: Invest in the American Funds, the low-cost leaders among load funds.)

Both no-load and load funds charge fees for managing your money, as well as various overhead expenses. Your total annual cost is called your *expense ratio.* No-load funds list their expense ratios online, compared with the average ratio for funds of that type. If you're buying a load fund, ask the salesperson for this same information. It's also in the prospectus (the document explaining the fund), but who looks?

Load funds carry higher expense ratios than no-loads do. For stock-owning load funds, the average is 1.75 percent a year, compared with 1.03 percent for no-loads (and 0.11 to 0.19 percent for the lowest-cost index funds—what a difference!). Because of all these expenses, broker-sold funds generally have poorer records than no-loads funds. It simply doesn't pay to buy mutual funds this way.

THE CASE AGAINST FINANCIAL PLANNERS WHO WORK ON COMMISSION

Most planners rely on sales commissions to earn their living. Others charge straight fees. Good fee-only planners can be a great help; you'll find out more about them in Chapter Eight. Planners who work on commission, however, have all the same conflicts of interest that stockbrokers do. They'll try just as hard to sell you a tax-deferred annuity or loaded mutual fund. If you want advice—and it's helpful, even comforting to have it—get it from someone whose standard of living doesn't depend on selling you something. Besides, with simple No Worry investing, you can advise yourself.

THE CASE AGAINST TRYING TO TIME THE MARKET

Market timers try to guess when stocks are going to rise and fall. They buy a stock fund when prices seem low and likely to rise. They hold it until they think prices are high and then they sell. After selling, they put the proceeds into a bond fund or money-market fund and wait for the next chance to buy.

On paper, this looks great. In practice, almost no one can do it consistently. You might buy at the right time, but sell too soon. When prices drop, you might wait too long before buying back. Prices might start up (so you buy), but then slide way down (scaring you into selling at a loss). The only people who jump in and out of the market at exactly the right time are *liars*. When markets go nowhere—rising and falling in a narrow range—it's tempting to try to time the cycles right. But as a long-term strategy, this doesn't work. What *does* work is rebalancing (page 183), which forces you to sell as prices rise and buy as prices fall. That's a form of market timing that's sensible and safe.

ARE THEY ALL WRONG?

I've been hard on money managers and financial salespeople here, so let me take a paragraph to explain myself. They're often smart (even very smart). They work hard. They're supported by state-of-the-art computer programs, Grade-A statistical work, and professional analysis. The good ones always do their best for customers. Some of them earn the money they're paid, especially when they help you with financial issues other than choosing investments. They give you comfort. But for long-term performance, they'll have a hard time doing better than my No Worry plans and will probably do worse. Aside from other considerations, their fees are too high. You can't beat the market when part of your gain is constantly being chipped away in costs. Just by choosing low-cost mutual funds, you'll retire with a lot more money to spend.

EXCHANGE-TRADED FUNDS

There's one more indexed product you might hear about. It's called an *exchange-traded fund* or *ETF* and tracks the performance of stock market indexes just the way index mutual funds do. These investments are fine for professionals, but they don't fit into most individual No Worry plans.

An ETF is a bundle of all the stocks in a particular index, such as the S&P 500. But instead of being sponsored by a mutual fund, it's structured as an individual stock. You buy and sell through a stockbroker or your online brokerage account, paying regular commissions on every trade. A Total Market ETF might work fine for a single chunk of money (such as an inheritance) that you want to hold for the long term. The annual fee is a hair less than you'd pay for most low-cost index funds. But an ETF is a poor choice for people making regular investments, because of the sales commission you'd have to pay each time. By contrast, it costs nothing to add money to a no-load mutual fund.

If you're curious about ETFs, look at the ones called Vipers that Vanguard sells (and read "Plain Talk on ETFs" at Vanguard .com). There are also "Spiders" (SPDRs, for Standard & Poor's Depository Receipts), which follow the S&P 500, and "Qubes" (QQQQs), which follow the speculative Nasdaq 100 index for high-tech companies. For lots of ETF information, see Morningstar .com.

TO SUM UP

Diversification, indexing, rebalancing—these three strategies make long-term investing work. The concepts are both sophisticated and simple. They're not exciting and aren't supposed to be. Investing should be about as thrilling as watching paint dry. It's the background to your life, not life itself.

But before you can turn your mind to other things, you have to get your new plan in place. Work from the list you made of all your current investments, moving the ones you circled for change. In your 401(k), switch to better funds and quit buying or holding company stock. Change the funds in your IRA or switch to an IRA that can give you what you want. Reconsider all the investments you hold outside your retirement plan. Ask yourself if you really want to work with a financial salesperson or whether it's smarter to own a few simple no-load, low-cost funds (you know my answer!).

Once you've started a No Worry plan, the biggest risk to your money will be what other people do. It's hard to resist investing with the herd. You'll hear someone praising her broker and wonder if you should do business there, too. You'll think about buying a telecom fund that your neighbor claims is making him 30 percent a year. Money managers sneer at index funds and dismiss one-choice funds with a sniffy, "One size can't fit all." Maybe not, but one size can fit 95 percent of us and I'm one of that 95 percent. I suspect that you are, too.

We all face the temptation of choice. Having lots of choices is supposed to be good because it puts you "in control." But when choices confuse you, you're not in control at all. In fact, you're at risk of making big investment mistakes. The No Worry choice puts you in maximum control. You've done the one thing that truly promises long-term success.

Once you've set up your plan, invest in it automatically—with payroll deductions or regular deductions from your bank account. Then sit back and let the paint dry. You've done all that's needed to provide a comfortable future for yourself.

8. WRAPPING UP

Keeping Score, Keeping Track, Keeping Cool

Finally, it's time to get organized. With any luck, you don't even have a lot to do. Remember—this is the *simple* life. You just need to set some goals and make a few phone calls. With the No Worry system, you know that you won't have overlooked anything important or chosen badly. You can set up this plan and let it run itself.

KEEPING SCORE

How do you know how well you're doing, financially? Only one way—by keeping score. Scorekeeping saves you from kidding yourself. You're either doing well or you're not. The way to tell is by measuring your *net worth*. Here's how to figure it:

List all the assets you own and their current value—your house, cars, retirement plans, bank accounts, and other investments. Then list all your liabilities (debts)—your mortgages, auto loans, credit-card debts, student loans, and any others. Subtract your liabilities from your assets. What's left is your net worth. It tells you how much wealth you'd actually hold in your hands if everything you owned were sold and all your loans paid off.

With careful, regular saving, investing, and debt repayments, your net worth should gradually go up (except in the occasional year when the stock market drops). If your net worth shrinks more than two years in a row, you're doing something wrong—borrowing too much, failing to save, or investing badly. Take a net-worth snapshot when you first set up your plan, to know your starting point. Every couple of years, on a rainy Saturday afternoon, get out your asset-and-liability list and update it. With No Worry saving and investing plus automatic debt repayments, your financial score should keep going up.

FINALLY, START YOUR FILING SYSTEM

For years, my filing system was a mess. I put things in piles, stored them in boxes, and accidentally threw important papers out. When I needed a document or had a question about my money, I had to excavate for hours. Twice, I lost the deed to my house and had to pay to have it replaced (my lawyer was in shock).

No more. My files are usually in order, except for the pile in the wire basket called "Waiting." I toss papers there when I'm busy or bored and file them when the pile tips past the basket's edge.

For keeping track of important papers, a filing cabinet helps. It doesn't have to be metal. A two-drawer cardboard file from an office-supply store will do, or even a cardboard storage box sized to hold manila file folders. Only two things matter: The box or cabinet has to be big enough for all your current records and it has to live in a place that's easy to get to. If you store it behind the junk in the closet under the stairs, you won't keep adding to it and your system will fall apart.

The labels on your files should be simple but exact so you can find things quickly. Instead of just calling a folder "Taxes," subdivide into "Taxes, federal," "Taxes, state," "Taxes, deductions" (for tax-deductible expenses and donations), and so on. A friend gave me a small labeling machine a few years ago and it changed my life. I *love* to make new file folders (it's a wonder I haven't labeled my drawers, light switches, bookshelves, and kids). Replacing the scrawl on my file folders with neat, clean printing even made my system easier to use, because I can read the tabs so quickly.

We'll all have different folders in our files, reflecting our different lives. But they'll almost certainly include the following (I've italicized the headings and subheadings):

Bank—files for Checking Account, Deposit Receipts, Savings Account, Credit Line, and Correspondence (for mail regarding your accounts, including printouts of e-mails)

Car—the Title and purchase papers or Lease Agreement

Cat—or dog, bird, ferret, orangutan, whatever

Credit Cards—for the PINs, fine-print agreements you sign, and photocopies of the cards you carry (in case they're lost)

Credit Reports—now that you'll be getting them free

Debts—the papers you signed for your Mortgage, Auto Loan, Home-Equity Loan, and Student Loan

Employee Benefits—for the information that your company sends

Home Purchase—the Deed and other legal documents

Income—for records of income not reported on a W-2, plus a copy of the year-end W-2 your employer sends

Insurance—files for Auto, Disability, Health, Homeowners or Renters, Other (such as insurance that comes with your credit card), and Correspondence

Instructions and Warranties—for all the digital stuff we can never remember how to operate (for computer manuals I finally got a plastic bin)

Investments—files for Mutual Funds, Retirement Plan, College Savings, Brokerage Account, Correspondence, and the Investment Plan you chose while reading Chapter Seven

Kids—for all the things a parent saves

Loans Made—for the records of any money owed you by someone else (easily forgotten, if something happens to you)

Memberships—for information from all the organizations you belong to

Master List—more about this below

Medical Bills—for bills you submit to your health insurer or to a Health-Care Savings Account for reimbursement; also for potential tax deductions

Military Records—including discharge papers and records of any benefits

Net Worth Statement—the score that shows how you're progressing over the years

Parents—for family information and parental finances that you may be responsible for

Passwords—for all your online accounts, or at least the ones you want your heirs to know about

Personal Papers—for birth, marriage, and death certificates, and family Social Security numbers; Adoption Papers; Divorce Agreement; Passports, and so on

Retirement Plans—for information on all your plans, including accounts that might be held with a former employer

Safe-Deposit Box—with a list of what's in the box and where the key is

Taxes—files for Federal, State, Deductions, and Correspondence, including your PIN if you file online

Travel—Dream Vacations; also, Old Vacations, in case you want to revisit where you've been

Will—for copies of your Living Will, Power of Attorney, and

Health-Care Power of Attorney, including the privacy waiver that lets your representative see your medical records.

Whys and Goals—a special word about this file: It's going to be your memory bank. As you've gone through this book and made financial choices, you've always thought about the reasons why. *Why* that particular investment, insurance policy, credit card, or savings plan is better for you than something else. You wrote down the "Why"—two or three sentences each time—and filed it in the proper folder, along with all the information about the financial product itself. For this final file, gather all those Whys together on a single sheet of paper. It's the Big Picture. You'll see your financial life whole, with all the parts relating. If a new "reason" comes into your life—marriage, children, job change, and so on—your Why file helps you apply that question to your entire financial life, to be sure that everything stays in balance. This is also the right file for the priority list of Goals (page 220).

When something enters your life that doesn't quite fit into a file you already have, start a new one. If you drop it into a file that's "almost" right, you're going to lose it. Your system should be so logical that anyone who needs to find something can lay hands on it immediately. Self-employment and home-business records need meticulous files all their own.

Once a year, I clean out my current file. Some things get tossed, such as quarterly investment statements and bank deposit receipts. Other items go into boxes for longer-term storage (those are the ones behind the junk in the closet under the stairs). My "keep" list includes bank statements, tax returns, receipts for tax-deductible items, year-end statements from mutual funds, old insurance policies (to prove I was covered), and important communications with insurance companies or banks. The IRS normally has three years from the date your tax return is filed to initiate an audit. So I keep my records for four calendar years, then throw them out. (Memo to, um, people with poor memories: If you under-report your income by more than 25 percent, the IRS has six years to find out. It can audit you anytime if you committed fraud or filed no tax return at all.)

YOUR MASTER LIST

Also make a special folder called Master List. I keep this list on my computer, with a printout in my files.

A Master List rounds up your entire financial life. It includes:

- Your bank accounts, the bank's phone number, and the name of any particular banker you deal with
- A list of your debts (you don't need the amounts, just the places you pay)
- The name, phone number, and e-mail of your insurance agent and the policies you hold
- The names of your mutual funds and their customer-service numbers
- The phone number of the employee-benefits office at work
- A list of your credit cards with the last four digits of each one's number, and the card company's customer-service phone
- A list of all your retirement plans and where they're located
- Your military service number and discharge date
- The name, phone number, and e-mail of your broker or planner
- The name, number, and e-mail of the lawyer who did your will
- Where to find the will, power of attorney, and health-care power of attorney
- The name, number, and e-mail of your tax preparer, if any
- Where to find the safe-deposit box (and key!)
- Information about any money owed you

- Information about any real estate you own, other than your home, plus the name, number, and e-mail of the person who looks after it
- Family Social Security numbers
- Passport numbers and expiration dates
- The combination of your home safe
- Et cetera

E-mail this list to a parent, one of your children, or your executor, so there's a copy somewhere else. Also, keep a copy in your filing cabinet. If something happens to you and (ahem) your filing system isn't perfect, this single sheet of paper will save your relatives untold time and trouble. If you have a fire and lose records, it will make life a whole lot easier for you, too. For security reasons, I don't include any account numbers or passwords in the file I keep on my computer. They're only in my paper file.

THE FILE FOR CURRENT BILLS

I don't bother with special file-cabinet folders for current bills. Instead, I use a simple accordion file labeled A through Z. When I pay a bill, I slip it into its alphabetical compartment where I can find it quickly if I need it. The only bills worth a place in your filing cabinet are those you can tax-deduct or the medical bills you're submitting to an insurer or Health Savings Account. At the end of each year, I stuff all the paid bills into a single manila file, I keep them a year, in case something comes up that I want to check (once in a blue moon, it does). Then I throw them out.

KEEPING YOUR PAPERS SAFE

Most financial documents can be replaced if a fire wipes them out. But it's a huge nuisance and, of course, you have to remember what they were. It's better to keep the critical ones in a fireproof home safe or a bank safe-deposit box. If you choose a safe, be sure that someone else knows the combination. If it's a safe-deposit box, give someone else the signature authority to get into the box if you're disabled. (You don't have to give that person the key. Just tell him or her where you keep it—and, please, keep it there!)

What might you put in a safe or safe-deposit box? The deed to your house, tax records for the past three years (they're a *real* pain to replace), account registration papers for mutual funds, savings bonds and any stock certificates you hold, copies of employment contracts, records of your retirement plans so that heirs won't lose track of them, your insurance policies, records of debts you've repaid and any money due you, the inventory you made of what's in your home (you did that, right?), an appraisal of your valuables, important jewelry you don't wear, copies of your will, living will, and power of attorney, personal papers that are time-consuming to replace, such as your birth certificate, marriage certificate, and military discharge papers, and a copy of your Master List.

And back up your computer files! I e-mail the most critical files to another location, just in case. While this book was in progress, I e-mailed the new work obsessively every night!

FILING EVERYTHING ON A FLASH DRIVE

If you're computer savvy, you can put your entire financial life on a tiny flash drive the size of your thumb. It pops into your pocket, if you have to flee your house ahead of a fire, landslide, hurricane, or buying expensive products containing high annual charges (some of them open, others hidden). Because of those charges, the products won't perform as well as you expect. All told, fee-based planners probably cost even more than you'd pay for fee-only advice. As just one example, say that you put $50,000 into a mutual fund with an upfront commission of $2,500 and another $600 in annual costs. That could buy 15 to 20 hours of a fee-only planner's time, plus a three-hour annual checkup. *And* you'd get better advice.

Commissioned planners don't think of their recommendations as biased. You asked for their advice and have to pay for it. Some of them suggest mutual funds that are lower in cost (principally, American Funds). But they might also sell you a high-cost annuity that you don't need. They have to push products to make a decent living—that's the way the business works. You'd do the same, if you had their jobs. But you don't have their jobs, so my best advice is to stay away.

How do you find a fee-only financial planner? Many of them don't take small accounts. They prefer clients who need more services or who have interesting amounts of money to manage (often $250,000 and up). Fortunately, growing numbers of fee-only planners are starting to work with people of lesser wealth or who are just starting out. There are three places to look:

1. The National Association of Personal Financial Advisors at Napfa.org—about 1,000 planners, in almost all states. To see if there are any near you, go to the website and type in your ZIP code. When names pop up, click on their profiles where they announce their specialties. Look for planners who say they serve middle-income client needs." If you don't see that phrase, email the nearby planners, explain the services you want, and ask if they offer advice by the hour. Some take hourly clients without advertising it. You can also get names of fee-only planners by mail. Call NAPFA at 800-366-2732.

flood. The flash drive might contain your Master List and any other important records that you keep on your computer. You could even scan your medical records, tax returns, car title, home deed, birth certificate, living will, and other important papers onto the drive. If you can't scan at home, take your documents to a copy center.

DO YOU NEED A FINANCIAL PLANNER?

Probably not. For most of us, planning is pretty simple: Spend less than you earn, work down your debts, build a Cushion Fund, take advantage of tax-deferred savings (401(k)s, Individual Retirement Accounts), and invest regularly in simple, low-cost mutual funds. You can manage all that yourself.

What planners *can* do is give you a kick, if you never seem to get around to fixing things yourself. You'll be paying for motivation (even a scolding), but when it works, it's worth every penny. Your planner will help you set financial goals, work out a sensible budget, improve your safety net, make better use of your employee benefits, and insist that you write a will. He or she will eyeball your tax return, to see if you've missed something obvious. You'll be shown how much more you ought to save, to reach an acceptable level of retirement income (hearing the message in person might be more effective than doing the Ballpark Estimate). A three-hour session can probably put you on track.

I can think of four particular times when a planner's advice (a *good* planner's advice) can be critical:

- If you inherit more money than you're accustomed to managing and want to be sure you don't squander it
- If you own a small business and need help with tax-deferred savings plans
- If you wonder whether you'll have enough money to retire

- If you're expecting a cash payout from your retirement plan and want to know how to make it last for life

Finding a Good Financial Planner

Anyone can claim to be a financial planner, so choose carefully. To start with, the planner should have one of two sets of initials after his or her name: CFP, for "Certified Financial Planner," someone who has taken the CFP course and passed the exam. Or CPA/PFS, for Certified Public Accountant/Personal Financial Specialist, a CPA with financial planning expertise. Neither set of initials is a guarantee of good advice and competence, but it clears the field.

There are two broad types of credentialed financial planners—the right kind and the wrong kind.

What's the right kind of planner? You want planners who charge only fees, not sales commissions. They advertise themselves as *fee-only* and typically belong to the fee-only National Association of Personal Financial Advisors. Their fee schedules vary. They may charge for their time—between $120 to $300 an hour. Some charge for specific projects or require annual retainers. If you want your investments managed, you'll typically pay 1 percent of the value of your account, per year. Fee-only planners usually put their clients' money into low-cost mutual funds—often, index funds—so as not to run up your expense. Many of them work with Vanguard or with Dimensional Fund Advisors, a group of index-like funds sold only through investment advisers.

What fee-only planners *don't* do is sell financial products, so you don't get biased investment advice. If he or she recommends a particular mutual fund or retirement account, you know it will be in your best interest, not because the planner expects to earn a commission. You should note one potential conflict: Some fee-only planners might urge you to let them manage your money (so they can earn 1 percent of your assets), when all you had in mind was a three-

hour checkup. But that's right on the surface and something you can control. There aren't any hidden payments flowing the planner's way.

What's the wrong kind of planner? A person who sells products and earn commissions. Here, you're at tremendous risk, even from planners who, personally, are sweetie-pies. The only way they can make a living is by selling you something. So they spend less time on budgeting and personal goals and more time promoting investment and insurance products that pay them well. If you say that you can't afford to make a significant purchase, they might "help" you find the money by advising that you stop contributing to your 401(k) (yikes!) or borrow against your house (double yikes!). They might show you computer printouts to "prove" that their way is better (I've seen some pretty biased printouts in my time). Their favorite products include high-cost mutual funds, wrap accounts, and annuities—all of them bad choices, compared with the low-cost well-diversified funds I suggested in Chapter Seven. The planne[rs] called Chartered Financial Consultants are all insurance age[nts] who will "solve" almost every planning problem with an insu[rance] policy or annuity. That's not advice, that's salesmanship.

Often, commissioned planners disguise the way they['re paid]. They may describe themselves as *fee-based* or *fee-offset[,]* think they're in the fee-only camp. They may even post [a sched]ule for various types of advice. When you visit, howeve[r,] that they reduce or eliminate fees if you decide to bu[y] products they recommend. In short, their fee sch[edule is essen]tially, a come-on. What they really want to do is s[ell,] where the money is.

You might imagine that commissioned plan[ners give good] advice because you don't have to write an act[ual check for their ser]vices. The planner might even tell you tha[t] ment—you get the help while the financial the cost. That's pure illusion. You pay—[and]

2. Garrettplanningnetwork.com, a network of about 250 planners in 41 states who work on an hourly basis with no minimum required. Their fees range widely. At this writing, the majority charge $180 to $210 an hour.

3. The Personal Financial Planning Center at http://pfp.aicpa .org—the site for Certified Public Accountants who are Personal Financial Specialists. Enter your area code or ZIP code, to get the names of local planners. Click on their names to see if they say they charge hourly fees. To get names of planners by phone, call 201-938-3828.

Most fee-only planners offer a get-acquainted session free. For the kinds of questions to ask, check the tips and brochures at Napfa.org.

If you can't find a fee-only planner, it's safer to manage your finances yourself. You don't want to risk running into a fee-based, fee-offset, or commissioned planner who sells poor investments. Certainly, many commissioned planners will treat you fairly, within the limits of their need to make a living. But if you don't know much about investing yourself, it's hard to tell good advice from bad. You'll be fine, if you let the summaries of each of these chapters be your guide.

DO YOU NEED A FINANCIAL PLAN?

A true financial plan shows you how you might handle your whole financial life. You fill out a worksheet for the planner, showing your income, outgo, savings, debts, investments, insurance, goals, expected retirement age, and so on. In return, you get a multipage document, sometimes in hard covers, showing you whether your current approach will meet those goals and, if not, what to do next.

The value of the plan, however, depends entirely on the planner.

A commissioned salesperson might produce a plan for $500 or so, but will use it principally as a sales tool. The plan will spotlight your "need" for the planner's annuities, mutual funds, IRAs, and other products. Run away, run away! If you've already paid for such a plan, chuck it and chalk it up to a lesson learned.

A fee-only planner will probably charge $1,500 and up for a comprehensive plan. But remember—you won't be urged to buy costly products you may not need. You'll spend more quality time on developing personal goals, with a spending and savings plan to match. You'll get help with employee benefits, taxes, and your 401(k). It might seem that you're paying the fee-only planner more, but because no commissions are ever charged, you'll usually wind up paying less. You should be steered toward better investments, too.

But do you really need a comprehensive plan? Unless you keep working with the planner, who will monitor what you do, that expensive proposal will probably land in the box in the closet under the stairs. Nothing will happen. You'll pretend it isn't there. For one-shot advice or a second opinion, you're better off with a two- or three-hour financial checkup. Your "plan" would be pretty straightforward, anyway, with the kind of advice you're been reading about here.

HOW ARE YOU GOING TO REACH YOUR GOALS?

Goals—specific, written goals—are a marvelous spur for getting your finances in order. If you float along with only general goals in mind, it's hard to focus your spending and saving on what really matters. That's what sets off the worry bug—the sense that you're going to run out of money just when you'll need it most.

For No Worry living, think about your lifetime goals and write them down. Put them in order, with the most important first. And make each goal specific. After reading this book, what, exactly, do you intend to do? What holes do you see in your finances that ought to be plugged? If you're married, you each should write a list, then negotiate your differences. Here's what your priorities might look like:

I Want . . .

1. *Full income protection against the unforeseen*—life, health, and disability insurance. Specifically, you might add: "Raise my life insurance to 10 times earnings and buy disability coverage."
2. *Full inheritance protection*—for my spouse, partner, or children. Specifically: "Call Tim, who knows a lawyer. Get an appointment to prepare a will, a power of attorney, a living will, and a health-care power of attorney."
3. *More money saved for retirement*—10 percent of earnings, with a plan for raising that to 15 percent and higher. Specifically: "Do the Ballpark Estimate. Raise the amount I'm contributing to my 401(k) and sign up for future, automatic increases, if that's allowed." Or, "Raise my 401(k) contribution by enough to get the full company match, but add nothing more until I wipe out my credit-card debt." Or, "Call a mutual-fund group such as Vanguard and start an IRA." Or, "Arrange to contribute to my IRA automatically every month." (You get the idea.)
4. *Better retirement investments*—mutual funds with superior prospects for long-term returns and less market risk. Specifically: "Check my 401(k) and switch to funds like the ones discussed in Chapter Seven." Or, "Choose better funds for my IRA." Or, "Quit buying my company's stock and sell the stock I have."
5. *Better use of employee benefits*—no more leaving free money or tax advantages on the table. Specifically: "See if my company

has a flexible spending plan for medical or child care benefits,
and sign up."

6. *No consumer debt*—an end to throwing money away on interest payments. Specifically: "Use Choosetosave.org (or another
calculator) to figure out what to pay each month to get rid of my
credit card debt." Or, "Charge only what I can pay in full each
month." Or "Pay for everything in cash for the next 12 months,
while I'm cleaning up my cards."

7. *A Cushion Fund*—for ready cash, to avoid scary scrambles for
money or loans. Specifically: "Figure out what I need to cover
three months' basic expenses. Set up a savings plan to achieve
it over the next 12 (or 24) months."

8. *A Happiness Fund*—to buy a house, take a vacation, redeco-
rate the living room, whatever. Specifically: "Figure out the
cost of 'whatever' and start saving for it."

9. *A college savings plan*—to provide children with at least some
help. Specifically: "Start a low-cost 529 plan to save enough for
a public college or university."

10. *More long-term investments*—for additional retirement savings, on top of a 401(k) or IRA. Specifically: "Start a Roth IRA,
using the types of funds suggested in Chapter Seven." Or,
"Start a new mutual-fund account." Or, "Start an IRA for my
spouse, who doesn't work outside the home."

Make all these payments automatic. As they start clicking in
you'll have less to spend on other things, *but that's the point*. You're
limiting casual spending (stuff you can do without) by putting
money into the things that matter more. And now that you have a
priorities list, you *know* what matters more. It's your message to
yourself.

You probably can't fund everything all at once, so start with the
things at the top of your list and gradually work down. If you're

paid twice a month, take your mortgage or rent out of one of the checks, your savings deposits out of the other, and debt-reduction payments out of both. Once you have your basic payments stabilized, you'll know what's going to be left in your checking account for other bills.

Put your Goals list in the Why file in your filing cabinet. That's your summary file, showing everything you've decided to do. But keep a copy on your desk or by your phone—somewhere right under your nose—where you can check off the jobs as you get them done. You might charge ahead and finish them all in a couple of weeks or work on them once a week and finish in two months. Note any changes you make as you go along and put them in the Why file, too. Then close the folder, give yourself a kiss, and get on with your real life.

Here's something that didn't go on my priority list: Live in a big house with a mortgage you can barely handle, take huge vacations that you can't pay for all at once, drive two (no, three!) expensive cars, and shop for a lot of stuff that eventually won't matter. Living large is no problem as long as you also have plenty of money to put away. But a lot of the people who live large are secretly living scared. They're running up debts and squirming when the bills come in. Where's the fun in that? Being able to pay your way with something left over—*that's* large, for me.

WHY YOU BOUGHT THIS BOOK

You want to be easy with your life. You'd like to spend your time getting better at your job, enjoying your family, seeing friends, playing tennis, or snoozing gently in your hammock with a book across your chest. You don't want to think about your money very much but know—for your own sake—that you have to handle it well. It's not hard, as you've seen. The principles are clear. Anyone can do it. I don't even have to wish you "good luck," because I know you'll be okay.

My First Rules

Only a few things work, and they work really well.

If you set up a system that runs automatically, you can't fail.

Success comes from starting right, then keeping your itchy fingers off.

My Last Rules

You can't see the future.

If you're saving money steadily, that doesn't matter.

All that really matters is getting more out of life.

Appendix:
The Ballpark Estimate®

This Estimate will show you roughly how much to save today in order to retire comfortably tomorrow. I know it works. I asked two leading planners to test it and they got results close to those their fancy computerized spreadsheets showed. No estimate will be exact. This paper-and-pencil version produces slightly different savings amounts from the Ballpark Estimate you'll find online at Choosetosave.org. But all you need is a target to get a good savings plan under way. My thanks to the Employee Benefit Research Institute and Research Fund and its American Savings Education Council program for letting me reproduce the Ballpark E$timate® here.

Get a Ballpark E$timate® of Your Retirement Needs.
The ChoosetoSave.org and American Savings Education Council's Planning and Saving Tool

Planning for retirement is not a one-size-fits-all exercise. The purpose of Ballpark is simply to give you a basic idea of the savings you'll need to make today for when you plan to retire.

If you are married, you and your spouse should each fill out your own Ballpark E$timate® worksheet taking your marital status into account when entering your Social Security benefit in number 2 below.

1. **How much annual income will you want in retirement?** (Figure at least 70% of your current annual gross income just to maintain your current standard of living; however, you may want to enter a larger number. See the tips below.)

$_____

(continued on next page)

Tips to help you select a goal:

→ 70% to 80% — You will need to pay for the basics in retirement, but you won't have to pay many medical expenses as your employer pays the Medicare Part B and D premium and provides employer-paid retiree health insurance. You're planning for a comfortable retirement without much travel. You are older and/or in your prime earning years.

→ 80% to 90% — You will need to pay your Medicare Part B and D premiums and pay for insurance to cover medical costs above Medicare, which on average covers about 55%. You plan to take some small trips, and you know that you will need to continue saving some money.

→ 100% to 120% — You will need to cover all Medicare and other health care costs. You are very young and/or your prime earning years are ahead of you. You would like a retirement lifestyle that is more than comfortable. You need to save for the possibility of long-term care.

2. **Subtract the income you expect to receive annually from:**

   • Social Security — If you make under $25,000, enter $8,000; between $25,000 - $40,000, enter $12,000; over $40,000, enter $14,500 (For married couples - the lower earning spouse should enter either their own benefit based on their income or 50% of the higher earning spouse's benefit, whichever is higher.)

   –$_____

   • Traditional Employer Pension — a plan that pays a set dollar amount for life, where the dollar amount depends on salary and years of service (in today's dollars)

   –$_____

   • Part-time income

   –$_____

   • Other (reverse annuity mortgage payments, earnings on assets, etc.)

   –$_____

   This is how much you need to make up for each retirement year:

   =$_____

Now you want a Ballpark E$timate of how much money you'll need in the bank the day you retire. For the record, we assume you'll realize a constant real rate of return of 3% after inflation and you'll begin to receive income from Social Security at age 65.

3. **To determine the amount you'll need to save, multiply the amount you need to make up by the factor below.**

Age you expect to retire:	Choose your factor based on life expectancy (at age 65):					
	Male, 50th percentile (age 82)	Female, 50th percentile (age 86)	Male, 75th percentile (age 89)	Female, 75th percentile (age 92)	Male, 90th percentile (age 94)	Female, 90th percentile (age 97)
55	18.79	20.53	21.71	22.79	23.46	24.40
60	16.31	18.32	19.68	20.93	21.71	22.79
65	13.45	15.77	17.35	18.79	19.68	20.93
70	10.15	12.83	14.65	16.31	17.35	18.79

$_____

4. If you expect to retire before age 65, multiply your Social Security benefit from line 2 by the factor below.

Age you expect to retire:	55	Your factor is: 8.8
	60	4.7

+$ _____

5. Multiply your savings to date by the factor below (include money accumulated in a 401(k), IRA, or similar retirement plan).

If you plan to retire in:	10 years	Your factor is: 1.3
	15 years	1.6
	20 years	1.8
	25 years	2.1
	30 years	2.4
	35 years	2.8
	40 years	3.3

–$ _____

Total additional savings needed at retirement: =$ _____

Don't panic. We devised another formula to show you how much to save each year in order to reach your goal amount. This factors in compounding. That's where your money not only earns interest, your interest starts earning interest as well, creating a snowball effect.

6. To determine the ANNUAL amount you'll need to save, multiply the TOTAL amount by the factor below.

If you want to retire in:	10 years	Your factor is: .085
	15 years	.052
	20 years	.036
	25 years	.027
	30 years	.020
	35 years	.016
	40 years	.013

=$ _____

EBRI
EMPLOYEE
BENEFIT
RESEARCH
INSTITUTE

2121 K Street NW
Suite 600
Washington, DC 20037
www.ebri.org
www.choosetosave.org

This worksheet simplifies several retirement planning issues such as projected Social Security benefits and earnings assumptions on savings. It reflects today's dollars; therefore, you will need to re-calculate your retirement needs annually and as your salary and circumstances change.

It also assumes that your wages will increase in the future at the same rate as inflation. This compares with the 2005 intermediate assumptions by the Social Security trustees that wages will increase 1.1 percentage points faster than inflation. Situations in which the wage growth is larger than the inflation rate will often require a higher rate of savings than this worksheet suggests. Unfortunately, a paper worksheet using an example where wage growth is not equal to inflation would be much more complicated.

Should you want a ballpark estimate that allows you to assume a wage growth that is different from the rate of inflation, you will need to go to http://www.choosetosave.org/ballpark and use the interactive ballpark estimate worksheet.

The American Savings Education Council (ASEC) mission is to make savings and retirement planning a priority for all Americans. ASEC is a program of the Employee Benefit Research Institute Education and Research Fund. For information on becoming an ASEC Partner, visit www.asec.org

Acknowledgments

My warmest thanks to the specialists in their fields who read this manuscript for accuracy and made many wise suggestions besides. My gurus include Robert Barney, the insurance expert behind Term4sale.com; investment consultant Charles Ellis, founder of Greenwich Associates and author of my investment bible, *Winning the Loser's Game;* Keith Gumbiner of Hsh.com, a consumer-friendly site loaded with mortgage information; mortgage virtuoso Jack Guttentag at Mtgprofessor.com, another great site for information; James Hunt, the life insurance actuary for the Consumer Federation of America and truly the consumer's friend; Joseph Hurley of Savingforcollege.com and the country's leading expert on 529 college savings plans; John Joyce, director of college planning services for the College Board and a super source on student financial aid; Charles Mandelstam and Norman Shaw, fine estate-planning attorneys at McLaughlin & Stern in New York City; Robert Manning, author of *Credit Card Nation*, who knows all the tricks of the credit-card trade; Stephen Moses, president of the Center for Long-Term Care Reform and urgent voice for understanding your old-age needs; and Larry Swedroe of Buckingham Asset Management, author of many books on the virtues of indexed investments.

Thanks, too, to Miriam Leuchter, Dori Perrucci, and Joan Raymond for research. Carll Tucker read the manuscript and made many helpful suggestions—especially helping me find the thread in the investment chapter. As always, I appreciate the support of my longtime agent Mort Janklow and dedicated (and persistent!) editor Alice Mayhew.

More than anything, this book owes its tone to my wonderful stepdaughter, Martha Quinn (you remember her from MTV!). Martha went over the manuscript sentence by sentence, asking me questions I hadn't thought about, rewriting sentences, pushing for clarity, and adding jokes. Thank you, Mar, for everything.

Index

About the Author

JANE BRYANT QUINN is the author of the bestselling *Making the Most of Your Money* and *Everyone's Money Book*. She writes regularly for *Newsweek* and *Good Housekeeping*. She lives in New York City.